FRANCIS

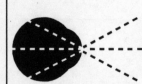

This Large Print Book carries the
Seal of Approval of N.A.V.H.

FRANCIS

MAN OF PRAYER

MARIO ESCOBAR

THORNDIKE PRESS

A part of Gale, Cengage Learning

Detroit • New York • San Francisco • New Haven, Conn • Waterville, Maine • London

GALE
CENGAGE Learning®

LIBRARY OF CONGRESS CATALOGING-IN-PUBLICATION DATA

Escobar, Mario.
　[Francisco. English]
　Francis : man of prayer / by Mario Escobar. — Large print ed.
　　pages cm. — (Thorndike Press large print biography)
　Originally published: Nashville, TN : Thomas Nelson, 2013.
　Includes bibliographical references.
　ISBN-13: 978-1-4104-6200-8 (hardcover)
　ISBN-10: 1-4104-6200-5 (hardcover)
　1. Francis, Pope, $d 1936– 2. Popes—Biography. 3. Large type books.
I. Title.
BX1378.7.E8313 2013
282.092—dc23　　　　　　　　　　　　　　　　　　2013019865

Published in 2013 by arrangement with Thomas Nelson, Inc.

Printed in the United States of America
1 2 3 4 5 6 7 17 16 15 14 13

For Elisabeth, Andrea, and Alejandro,
my best decision

CONTENTS

ACKNOWLEDGMENTS

We writers try to be geniuses with our words, but there are publishers who are geniuses with their thoughts and ideas. Larry A. Downs is that kind of man. Thank you, Larry, for the connection we have despite the thousands of miles between us.

My deep admiration goes to the teams of Grupo Nelson and Thomas Nelson. They can work miracles, as I have witnessed over the past few weeks: Graciela Lelli, conductor of the orchestra, able to keep her cool in the midst of incredible stress — I remember that walk on the beach in Miami with your shoes in your hand and your head in a book. Juan Carlos Martín Cobano is the kind of person who looks at things and sees what the rest of us mortals cannot — good work, my friend. Gretchen Abernathy, whom I have just recently gotten to know, is the perfect bridge between two cultures, meticulous and tireless — I hope to meet you in person. If there is any error in this book, it is entirely my own. Anything good is a result of these three geniuses.

The entire team of Thomas Nelson has worked ceaselessly. Thanks to Paula Major who has put up with this Spaniard and his literary hang-ups. Matt Baugher, thank you for betting on this book and taking it to the ends of the earth.

Thank you to Roberto Rivas, my Mexican friend, for believing so much in my books.

And I cannot forget the good work of the Silvia Bastos Literary Agency and the indefatigable Pau Centellas, who receives my countless e-mails with thousands of ideas. Thank you, Pau, for supporting me in everything. And thank you to Robert Downs for releasing this book to the entire world.

INTRODUCTION

It is one of the most impressive ceremonies in the world: one hundred fifteen cardinals process from the Pauline Chapel under Michelangelo's stunning frescos through the Sala Regia to seal themselves within one of the most beautiful rooms ever made by human hands, the Sistine Chapel. There they remain until, inspired by the Holy Spirit, they name the man who will lead the Catholic Church.

The cardinals proceed in order to the entrance of the Sistine Chapel and take their places. They sing the *Veni Creator,* an ancient prayer to invoke the Holy Spirit. They then swear, one by one, to closely observe the rules of the conclave. These rules can be reduced to two: 1) to faithfully fulfill Peter's mandate if they are elected pope and 2) not to reveal the secrets related to the pontiff's election.

Once the ceremony of oaths has concluded, the Master of Papal Liturgical Celebrations orders in Latin, *"Extra omnes!"* which means "Everyone else, out!" The doors slam shut, and the cardinals begin their discussion.

Within the walls of Vatican City, time seems to stand still; the urgency and agitation of the modern world are nearly unthinkable in this, the world's smallest state. Beyond the walls the commotion of over six thousand journalists and photographers with their cameras, all eager to be the first to capture a picture or file a report on the newly elected pope, remains distant to this most important religious meeting.

When the much anticipated *fumata bianca,* "white smoke," rises from the chimney of the Sistine Chapel, the excitement among the crowds in St. Peter's Square explodes into a great festival of the faith for Catholics. Television, radio, and newspaper media around the globe anxiously await the appearance of the new pope in the central balcony. Meanwhile, the new pope prepares himself in the Room of Tears, where, before revealing himself to the world, he undresses before God.

After a brief interval, which for many believers around the world feels interminable, the newly elected pope greets the worldwide Catholic Church. He raises his voice and pronounces the *Urbi et Orbi* ("to the City [Rome] and to the World") blessing. St. Peter's Square resounds with a deafening clamor, and much of the world studies the face of the new pope from television and computer screens.

When Pope Francis, the Cardinal Jorge Mario Bergoglio, with arms uplifted and palms open to the crowd, spoke his first words, St. Peter's Square grew instantly silent:

Brothers and sisters, good evening!

You know that it was the duty of the Conclave to give Rome a Bishop. . . . The diocesan community of Rome now has its Bishop. . . .

I would like to give the blessing, but first — first I ask a favour of you: before the Bishop blesses his people, I ask you to pray to the Lord that he will bless me: the prayer of the people asking the blessing for their Bishop.[1]

Not long ago Pope Francis had been virtually unknown, not only to the world but also to the vast majority of Catholic believers. So many questions and doubts have arisen regarding the direction he will take the

Catholic Church in the next few years: Will Pope Francis be the one to bring the Catholic Church into the twenty-first century? Will he become the first to authorize the marriage of priests? How will he handle the scandals that have beleaguered the Catholic Church in the past few years? Will Pope Francis maintain his stance of support for the poor? Will he encourage greater inter-religious dialogue?

To answer these and other questions, this book will delve into the life, words, and thoughts of one of the most powerful men on earth.

The background of Jorge Mario Bergoglio, the first Latin American to be named pope, will reveal the influences that have shaped him throughout his extensive ecclesiastical and personal life. His formation as a Jesuit and his academic concentrations in the world of science and letters, his ecumenical disposition toward other faiths, his willingness to dialogue with other religions, and his commitment to help the poor will all undoubtedly leave their mark on the third pontificate of the twenty-first century and of the new millennium.

Pope Francis's words in one of his first declarations as pope could not be more straightforward:

Those words came to me: the poor, the poor. Then, right away, thinking of the poor, I thought of Francis of Assisi. Then I thought of all the wars, as the votes were still being counted, till the end. Francis is also the man of peace. That is how the name came into my heart.[2]

Shy, aloof, a man of few words, he flees the pursuit of a career; yet it is precisely that quality which is considered one of his greatest merits. His austerity and frugality, together with his intense spirituality, are details that increasingly make him a candidate for the papacy.

— SANDRO MAGISTER, VATICAN EXPERT, *L'ESPRESSO*[1]

Pope Francis is a Jesus Christ–centered man who reads the Bible every day.

— LUIS PALAU, PASTOR AND EVANGELIST[2]

On behalf of the American people, Michelle and I offer our warm wishes to His Holiness Pope Francis as he ascends to the Chair of Saint Peter and begins his papacy. . . . As the first pope from the Americas, his selection also speaks to the strength and vitality of a region that is increasingly shaping our world, and alongside millions of Hispanic Americans, those of us in the United States share the joy of this historic day.

— BARACK OBAMA, PRESIDENT OF THE UNITED STATES OF AMERICA[3]

I wish the new Pope elect, His Holiness Francis, much light and positive energy for leading the Catholic people.

— LIONEL MESSI, ARGENTINE SOCCER PLAYER[4]

Years ago, to our great shame, we attended luxurious dinners at Cáritas where jewelry and other ostentatious luxuries were raffled off. You were wrong: that is not Cáritas.

— POPE FRANCIS, 2009 CÁRITAS NATIONAL ASSEMBLY[5]

These are the hypocrites of today: those who 'clericalize' the church, those who draw the people of God away from salvation. And that poor girl who, though she could have sent her son back to his maker, had the courage to bring him into the world and now goes from parish to parish trying

18

to get him baptized.

— POPE FRANCIS, CLOSING MASS, 2012 *PASTORAL URBANA* CONFERENCE[6]

We priests tend to 'clericalize' the laity. And the laity — not everyone, but many people — beg us on their knees to clericalize them because it is more comfortable to be an altar boy than a protagonist on the lay road. We do not have to fall into this trap. It is sinful complicity. . . . Lay people are laity and have to live as laity in the strength of baptism . . . carrying their daily cross just like we all do. They carry the cross of the laity, not of the priest. The cross of the priest should be born by the priest since God has given him a broad enough shoulder for it.

— POPE FRANCIS, NOVEMBER 2011[7]

■ ■ ■ ■

PART I
THE SPRING DAY
THAT CHANGED
MY LIFE

■ ■ ■ ■

CHAPTER 1
THE LANGUAGE OF
HIS MEMORIES

A FAMILY OF ITALIAN IMMIGRANTS

When I was thirteen months old, my mother had my second brother; there are five children in all. My grandparents lived nearby, and to help my mother out, my grandmother would come get me in the morning, take me to her house, and bring me back in the afternoon. They spoke Piedmontese to each other, and I learned it. They loved all my siblings, of course, but I had the privilege of entering the language of their memories.[1]

The story begins in 1934, in the Salesian prayer chapel of San Antonio, in the neighborhood of Almagro in Buenos Aires. A young man of Italian origin named Mario José Bergoglio and a young woman named Regina María Sívori, also of Italian background, stole secret glances at each other while the priest celebrated mass. In something of a premonition, one year later the couple married and started what would eventually become a family of five children, the oldest of whom would become the future Pope Francis.

Mario José Bergoglio came from a well-to-do family in Piedmont, Italy. His father ran a candy store in Portacomaro, in northern Italy. Europe was still trying to heal from World War I, and a devastating economic crisis was about to hit around the world.

Toward the end of 1928, the Bergoglios boarded the ship *Giulio Cesare,* and one hot morning in January 1929, they finally glimpsed the port of Buenos Aires. Jorge Mario's grandfather was hoping to reunite with his three brothers who had been running a pavement business in Paraná since 1922.

Their beginnings in Argentina could not have been more promising. The recently arrived family settled in the Bergoglio palace, a luxurious four-story residence with the only elevator in the city. The immigrant family lived on one of the floors and began working in the family business.

The crisis of 1929 was slow to hit the prosperous Argentina, but in 1932, the Bergoglios had to sell the family home. One of the brothers went to Brazil to seek his fortune; another died of cancer, and while

Jorge Mario's grandfather tried to stay afloat, his father had to seek work elsewhere. He was finally able to find a job with a new business and worked as an accountant for the company.

A Peaceful Life

Jorge Mario Bergoglio did not live through those years of crisis, but a new specter was beginning to emerge on the international scene: Nazism. Bergoglio was born in 1936, when it seemed as if the world was gradually recovering from the Great Depression.

Jorge Mario's family was modest and never faced great hardships. His grandmother, of whom he has fond memories, instilled the Piedmontese spirit of the family into her grandson, tying the immigrant child to his Italian roots. His father took all the children to watch him play basketball in the club of San Lorenzo. Both his parents played cards with the five children, and his mother cultivated their interest in opera. On Saturday afternoons they all would listen to public radio, and Regina would float away with the music as her children watched, entranced.

Jorge Mario's father also cooked. As a result of complications in the delivery of her fifth child, Regina suffered from a degree of paralysis, so Mario José had to prepare the food. While his wife gave him instructions on how to cook their delicious Italian meals, the children paid close attention to the recipes, and eventually everyone learned to cook a few dishes. Jorge Mario even became something of a chef when he lived at the Máximo school of San Miguel and cooked every Sunday for the students.

Though the Bergoglio family enjoyed a comfortable life without economic hardship, Mario José thought it best for his oldest son to learn the value of hard work and sacrifice. When Jorge Mario finished primary school, his father encouraged him to find a job. As Pope Francis recalled, his father said, "Look, since you're about to start high school, you need to start working. Over your break I'm going to find something for you to do."[2]

His father's suggestion came as a surprise. The family could not afford the luxuries of owning an automobile and taking lavish vacations, but it was far from needing an extra salary. Jorge Mario spent a few years cleaning the offices where his father worked as an accountant, and during his third year of high school, he assumed administrative duties. By his fourth year he was juggling work hours with trade school and time in the lab. The young student was in the office from 7:00 a.m. to 1:00 p.m., then dashed off to school, ate on the run, and did not return home until his classes ended at 8:00 p.m.

The experience toughened up the young man who, once he became cardinal, reflected on what he had learned during those years: "I'm so grateful that my father made me work. Work was one of the things that improved me in life. In the lab especially I learned the good and the bad of human effort."[3]

The Argentine adolescent learned the value of work, and his work ethic has made him indefatigable. Regarding the value of work, Pope Francis remarked:

Neither inheritance, family upbringing, nor education bestow the anointing of dignity. It only comes through work. We eat what we earn; we maintain our family with what we earn. It matters not if it is much or little. If it is much, all the better. We might have a fortune, but if we do not work, dignity crumbles.[4]

Friends and schoolmates in the Buenos Aires neighborhood of Flores remember him during those juvenile years. Amalia, one of his childhood friends and perhaps his first girlfriend when they were twelve or thirteen years old, told several journalists that the young Jorge Mario came to ask her hand in marriage.[5] She said that her suitor told her that if he did not marry her, he would become a priest.

Susana Burel, one of his neighbors, told the EFE News Agency that Jorge Mario was "studious and full of curiosity. He was raised in a good home, and that's key; the family is very important."[6]

Located near the Antonio Cerviño public high school, where he studied and proved to be a model student, is the parish of Santa Francisca Javier Cabrini. Jorge Mario officiated his first mass there when he was regional vicar in his neighborhood of Flores.

Bergoglio's early life was relatively peaceful and simple, as was life for most adolescents in Buenos Aires in the 1950s. The world was slowly healing from World War II, but the Cold War was on the rise. Juan Domingo Perón governed a prosperous Argentina, which, thanks to the war, had recovered its industry and commerce. The city of Buenos Aires grew ever larger and more beautiful, becoming known as the "Great" Buenos Aires. Meanwhile, one restless youth walked the streets with his heart torn between a girl and his priestly vocation. Unbeknownst to him, he was about to make a decision that would change his plans for the future and set him on a course to make history.

Chapter 2
That Spring Day
VOCATION AND SURRENDER

In that confession, something strange happened to me. I don't know what it was, but it changed my life; I would say that it caught me with my guard down. . . . It was the surprise, the astonishment of the encounter. I realized that they were waiting for me. That is what religious experience is: the shock of finding yourself with someone who is waiting for you. From that moment on, for me, God is the one who seeks you first.[1]

The *Día de la primavera,* "first day of spring," is a popular and important holiday in Argentina, celebrated on September 21. That afternoon in 1953, Jorge Mario Bergoglio tidied himself up a bit more than usual. He was going to see his girlfriend. But on the way something must have occurred to him. He began to worry, and stopping at the church in San José de Flores, he decided to go to confession.

The brief exchange between the priest and the young man led to a radical change in Jorge Mario's life. The decision to become a priest was not an easy one to make. It meant abandoning his entire life and giving up the dream of having a family. Jorge Mario Bergoglio was only sixteen years old, and he had a girlfriend. With a promising future ahead of him, he could be a respectable Catholic without becoming a priest. Yet on that bright spring afternoon he felt what he beautifully describes as a spiritual calling: "God is the one who seeks you first. You are looking for him, but he finds you first. You want to find him, but he has already found us."[2]

Bergoglio has referred frequently to this unexpected encounter with God. In the book he coauthored with Abraham Skorka, Bergoglio remarked on religious vocation, "Instead, everything happens from being called, summoned, touched by God."[3]

A short time after making his decision for the priesthood, Jorge Mario Bergoglio broke up with his girlfriend. He knew that God was calling him to a ministry and that his life had to change. But wanting to be completely sure, he took his time before entering seminary.

When he told his parents of his new plans,

he was surprised that his father supported him unconditionally while his mother disagreed with him. She wanted Jorge Mario, the eldest boy, to finish his degree, and she was tormented by feelings of losing her son forever. His grandmother was much more understanding. He recalled her words: "Well, if God calls you, go with our blessing. . . . Please, never forget that the doors of this house are always open and nobody will blame you if you decide to come back."[4]

Jorge Mario's grandmother was exemplary in wisdom. Her advice helped shape his ability to support and counsel the people who eventually sought his help in making important decisions in their lives.

Before starting seminary Bergoglio finished his studies and training in the lab. He breathed not a word about his vocational plans to the people around him as his thoughts formulated within. He slowly began to step back, desiring a purposeful solitude to help him solidify his plans.

The four years before he entered seminary were a time of great reflection. During that period he formed his political identity and studied certain cultural matters that greatly interested him. When he finally took the next step, Jorge Mario had experienced what life outside of religious service was like, and he had something with which to compare life inside the Catholic Church. While there is no proof to support their claims, some have asserted that in this time frame he flirted with politics and was active in Peronist youth movements, similar in many ways to fascist Italian youth movements.

The Decision

At age twenty-one, Bergoglio entered seminary and chose the Order of the Jesuits. He first enrolled in the archdiocesan seminary of Buenos Aires but was eventually drawn to the seminary of the Society of Jesus.

In the second part of this book, the Society of Jesus is discussed in depth, but it is worth mentioning here the incredible power and prestige that the Society of Jesus has had in Latin America. It was the followers of St. Ignatius of Loyola who served as the pope's army to stop the Protestant Reformation in Europe and as a tremendous evangelizing force throughout Asia and the Americas. That small group of priests, who used their famous spiritual exercises to seek an encounter with God through a personal spiritual experience, became the cultural elite and the pope's vanguard. They have always followed the pope in absolute obedience.

Jorge Mario Bergoglio recognized that what most attracted him to the Society of Jesus was the discipline it required:

Honestly I didn't really have a clue what direction to go in. What was clear was my religious vocation. In the end, . . . I joined the Society of Jesus, attracted by how they are a force for advancing the Church, speaking in military terms, growing through obedience and discipline. And therefore they are oriented toward missionary work. Over time, I wanted to go on mission to Japan, where the Jesuits have been doing very important work for a long time. But because of the severe health problems I've had since I was young, I wasn't allowed to go. Quite a few people would've been free of me if I'd been sent over there, wouldn't they?[5]

The first few years in seminary were hard for the young Jorge Mario. His mother did not accompany him to enroll that first year. She later became used to her son's vocation but only from a distance. When he was ordained as a priest, she attended the ordination and, at the end of the ceremony, knelt to ask for his blessing.

Through it all, as Jorge Mario Bergoglio recounted to the journalist Sergio Rubin, God's calling was irresistible:

Religious vocation is God's calling on a heart that is waiting for it, knowingly or not. I've always been struck by a reading from the breviary that says that Jesus looked at Matthew with an expression that, when translated, would be something like "mercying" and choosing. That is precisely how I felt God was looking at me during that confession. And that's the way he always asks me to look at others: with great mercy and as if I were choosing them for him; not excluding anyone, because all are chosen to love God. "Mercying and choosing him" was the theme of my consecration as bishop and is central to my religious experience.[6]

One of Pope Francis's ideas about vocation, or God's calling, comes from the prophecies of Jeremiah and his vision of the branch of an almond tree, the first to flower in spring (Jer. 1:11). Another is from a paraphrase of the apostle John: "God loved us first; love consists of this, that God loved us first."[7]

To find God, we must stop and listen. There is no other way. Young Bergoglio came to this understanding of God as he sought a haven for rest. For him, prayer is far from being merely a way of asking God for things. Prayer, above all, is a form of submission. When we admit our powerlessness, God acts in our lives.

EDUCATION

Jorge Mario Bergoglio has always had a deep appreciation for being knowledgeable. His educational background is well-rounded, and he is, in a way, a man of both science and letters. He has been both a student and a strict professor.

At the beginning of his ecclesiastical career, Bergoglio had to face a difficult lesson, perhaps the most difficult of all: pain. Fearing death during a long, agonizing illness that included high fevers, he clung to his mother and anxiously asked what was happening to him. The doctor, however, had no diagnosis for his illness, so his mother could not answer her son's fearful question.

Many times in the face of pain we ask, why? Why am I suffering? Why do I have to die? Why did these people I love so much have to die and in such a painful way? Humans want to discover the reason for their suffering. Yet God seems to be focused less on why and more interested in our reactions to pain.

Jorge Mario was suffering intense, unbearable pain. At age twenty-one he was a strong young man who felt God's calling on his life. Yet this same God seemed to have thrown him onto a bed of agony. Bergoglio said those who came to see him in the hospital repeatedly said things were going to get better, that his pain would go away, yet their words held little comfort for him. Then a nun he had known since he was a child said something that quieted both his body and soul. "She told me something that really stuck with me and gave me a lot of peace. She said I was imitating Jesus."[8]

Jorge Mario was learning the most important lesson of his life: pain and suffering draw us closer to God. Through the incarnate Jesus Christ, God had suffered. How then could the future pope ask for a life without suffering? Physical limitation stayed with him the rest of his life and ended his hopes of mission work in Japan, but it showed him a path that he would otherwise never have trod. He expressed it in the following words:

Pain is not a virtue in and of itself, but

37

the way we deal with it can be virtuous. Our vocation is fullness and joy, and along the way, pain is a border, a limiting factor. Therefore, we understand the sense of pain in fullness through the pain of God in Christ.[9]

Bergoglio's words seem out of place today. We live in a hedonist society in which pleasure seems to be the only goal of humanity. People constantly anesthetize themselves to both physical and emotional pain. Yet when we lose the capacity to feel pain and suffering, we cease to be truly human. Though perhaps one of the least publicized, this is one of the greatest teachings of Christianity.

The other great lesson Bergoglio learned through this experience was not to wallow in the pain. In view of what Christ underwent on the cross, there is a resurrection for Christians after the pain. As he described it, "That's why I think the key is to understand the cross as a seed of resurrection. Every attempt to endure pain produces only partial results unless it is based on transcendence."[10] His theological education taught him how to construct and order this experience, but it could not provide the experience.

Bergoglio first studied in the Jesuit seminary of Santiago, Chile, which was located in the old retreat house of San Alberto Hurtado. This was a special place for the Jesuits. San Alberto Hurtado was a Chilean Jesuit who founded the *Hogar de Cristo,* "Home of Christ." Besides being a well-known Jesuit, Hurtado spent his life improving the situation of Chilean workers. His spiritual director, the Jesuit Fernando Vives, had taught him the importance of social responsibility.

San Alberto Hurtado studied law at the Pontifical Catholic University of Chile and later entered politics, belonging to the Conservative Party. Pouring a great deal of his life into young people, the Jesuit ended up founding a union called *Acción Sindical y Económica Chilena* (Chilean Union and Economic Action), which some accused of being communist. The Chilean government memorialized the day of his death as the Day of Solidarity, and Pope John Paul II beatified him in 1994.

Studying in this institution, founded by and dedicated to San Alberto Hurtado, clearly influenced Jorge Mario Bergoglio's focus on the poor and on social justice. In the seminary in Santiago, Chile, the future pope received a classical education and studied Latin, history, Greek, and literature. After his time in the seminary and his ordination as a priest, he traveled to Spain to continue his studies in Alcalá de Henares. He studied theology from 1967 to 1970.

Bergoglio combined many of his years of study with teaching. From 1964 to 1965 he taught literature and philosophy at the *Colegio de la Inmaculada de Santa Fe* (Santa Fe School of the Immaculate One), and in 1966 he taught the same subjects in the *Colegio del Salvador de Buenos Aires* (Buenos Aires School of the Savior). One of his students, Jorge Milia, told a story of how strict Bergoglio could be as an educator. When another student had not done his homework, the young Jesuit teacher Bergoglio called on that student to teach the lesson:

"You're going to teach the entire lesson," the teacher told him. "They're going to crucify you," a classmate whispered. The student did a marvelous job of teaching the lesson, but everyone feared that it would not be enough to pacify Jorge Mario Bergoglio, who took teaching very seriously. At the end, Bergoglio told him, "You should get a ten, but we have to give you a nine, not to reprimand you but to remind you always that what matters is doing your duty day by day; doing your work systematically without letting it become a mere routine; building brick by brick instead of a fit of improvisation that so easily seduces."[11]

The educational philosophy of hard work defines the new pope. The final result matters less than the process that leads to that outcome. If we cannot create good habits, what we achieve in life matters little.

Bergoglio has spoken of a rich and famous Argentine businessman he happened to meet on a flight. When they arrived at their destination, the baggage was delayed, and this man began to get angry and yell — did they not know who he was, they could not treat him like this, and so on. Bergoglio reflects that a man who has achieved great things in life but is unable to control himself has lost all moral authority over others.[12] Doubtless, the new pope will be self-controlled, patiently achieving what he seeks without neglecting the processes and norms.

HOW TO MAKE A JESUIT

Bergoglio's background as a Jesuit has a great deal to do with his character. In the book he coauthored with his friend Rabbi

Skorka, Bergoglio defined the four pillars in the education of Catholic seminarians, particularly the Jesuits. He explained the first in his simple words:

> The first pillar is spiritual life, where the candidate enters into dialogue with God in his interior world. Therefore, the first year of education is dedicated to learning and practicing a life of prayer, a spiritual life. The rest that follows is less intense.[13]

Spiritual life is the center that drives the life of the priest. Bergoglio, a man of prayer, understands this very clearly, and with this first pillar refers to creating habits, not just principles or theological knowledge, that help the priest throughout his entire ministry.

The second pillar involves community life. Humans are social beings, and Bergoglio believes those who are going to serve the church and society ought to develop the empathy to put themselves in the place of their neighbors and live with and for them.

> We are not meant to be educated in solitude. We must be "kneaded" and grow within a community so we can

later bear it up and lead it. This is why our seminaries exist. In every community competition and jealousy exist, and this helps polish the heart and teach us to yield to others. These situations arise even in soccer games among the seminarians.[14]

The priest and the seminarian have to learn to live together and develop these habits in community. Priests preside over parishes and need to know how to resolve conflicts and negotiate with others. From the beginning, Christianity has been communal: from the book of Acts to the *comunidades de base* (grassroots communal movements) in modern parishes or in Protestant churches, where everyone knows each other and helps each other.

Bergoglio never idealizes seminary or the priesthood. Since seminarians are men with passions and weaknesses as all other men, it is to be expected that conflicts arise as they live together. Therefore, the second pillar in Jesuit formation is living together in communal life as a habit for pastoral ministry.

The third pillar Jorge Mario Bergoglio addressed is intellectual life. Though modern society would perhaps value this one above the others, he placed it third. For six years seminarians study theology — how to explain God, the Trinity, Jesus, and the sacraments — as well as the Bible and moral theology. The first two years are spent studying philosophy, to aid in better understanding theology throughout the rest of their education.

The fourth pillar Bergoglio mentioned is apostolic life. To learn how to be a pastor, seminarians spend the weekends in a parish church, helping the priest and learning from him. In their final year of seminary, they live in a parish. Throughout this year of testing, the supervisors observe the virtues and defects of the aspiring priests.

These four pillars are to mold priests, and in a certain sense they should be the model for every Christian. Spiritual life, community life, intellectual formation, and ministry are the foundation for a life of faith.

Though a university degree is not required for priesthood, it is very rare to find a Jesuit without one. Because of their teaching vocation, Jesuits tend to dedicate a great part of their lives to education. Furthermore, Jesuits have always been the elite of the Catholic Church, especially in the area of apologetics.

Pope Francis has an expansive and thorough educational background, with his studies of chemistry, his time in seminary, his study of humanities in Chile, and his advanced *licenciatura* degree in humanities from the *Colegio Mayor de San José* (Fraternal School of San José). He also has a *licenciatura* in theology and has taught various subjects for several years. Bergoglio finished his doctoral thesis in Germany.

From 1980 to 1986, he was the school president of the *Colegio Máximo* (Máximo School) and the *Facultad de Filosofía y Teología de la Casa San Miguel* (School of Philosophy and Theology of Casa San Miguel). His solid background and service in education later complemented his service in various positions within the Catholic Church of Argentina.

CHAPTER 3
DIFFICULT DAYS OF DICTATORSHIP

We are all political animals, in the uppercase sense of the word *politics.* We are all called to political action in the construction of our people.[1]

The twentieth century in Argentina, as in many Latin American nations, was characterized by dictatorships. Military coup d'états and the army's invasion of civil life, especially in violent ways, were constant.

The first dictatorship of the twentieth century in Argentina began in the 1930s under Uriburu and was followed by a severe economic crisis. In 1943, the upper echelons of the military organized another coup, the self-proclaimed Revolution of '43. This dictatorship ended with the rise to power of Juan Domingo Perón, perhaps the most famous Argentine politician.

Peronism was a political phenomenon that pervaded the rest of the twentieth century, taking different forms of government and social policy. The movement always retained a clear populist focus and widespread support among the poorest sectors. The rise in politics of Perón's wife, Eva Perón, allowed Argentine women to enter politics and become more visible in society.

In 1962, a new coup d'état lead to the dictatorship of José María Guido. This case was exceptional in that the coup was led by a civilian rather than a member of the military. This dictatorship eventually fell to another military uprising. Only four years later another coup occurred, this time headed by military leader Juan Carlos Ongania. This coup was also called the Argentine Revolution.

The worst of the dictatorships, the one that left the most lasting mark on the country, began in 1975, with the self-titled National Reorganization Process. The coup d'état of March 24, 1976, overturned the government of María Estela Martínez de Perón. The six year dictatorship of Jorge Rafael Videla that followed held a degree of repression and cruelty never before seen in Argentina.

Kidnapping and murdering dissidents was a common practice, as was the systematic stealing of children born to prisoners and their subsequent adoption by families within the dictatorial regime. In the name of liberalism and making a stand against communism, Jorge Rafael Videla and his supporters carried out a true reign of terror. The regime enjoyed strong support from the Catholic Church of the day, though one of the groups most at odds with Videla's rule was the Society of Jesus.

Curiously, as already mentioned regarding the Society of Jesus in Chile, the society in Argentina and other Latin American countries as well began a leftward leaning that led to revolutionary positions and postures of social struggle. The work of San Alberto Hurtado in Chile, as previously discussed, led the Society of Jesus to focus more and more on the struggles of the poor and the working class.

In 1954, Pope Pius XII ordered all working priests back into the parishes and requested that they cease their political militancy.[2] Nonetheless, this did not inhibit the development a few years later of what became known as liberation theology. Liberation theology originated in Brazil and grew out of Catholic grassroots movements that sought a more just society. In 1957, a consciousness-raising movement began in Brazil. Priests began politically educating the disenfranchised classes and helping them achieve literacy.

The year 1965 saw the birth of the First National Pastoral Plan in Brazil. The arrival of two European priests at this moment of political evolution was key to the development of liberation theology. Emmanuel Suhard, from France, and the Dominican Jacques Loew began working in the factories to see what life was like for Brazil's working class. The ideology of liberation theology holds to the basic principles of a preferential option for the poor, the marriage of Christian salvation with social and economic freedom, and the elimination of exploitation, among other ideas.

When Videla's dictatorship began in 1976, Jorge Mario Bergoglio was already a provincial superior of the Society of Jesus in Argentina. The provincial superior is an office appointed directly by the superior general of the Society of Jesus in Rome. The post can be held for only a few years, and its authority over the people in its charge is similar to that of a bishop within the hierarchy of the Catholic Church. The responsibilities of a Jesuit provincial superior include visiting members and organizing and presiding over the provincial chapter.

Jorge Mario Bergoglio was the provincial

superior throughout the harshest years of the dictatorship, during which time two Jesuits were kidnapped. Bergoglio had asked two of the Jesuits most active in the class struggles, Orlando Yorio and Franz Jalics, to desist in their labors in the shantytowns of the poor, but they refused. Bergoglio, along with others in the Society of Jesus, was not entirely in agreement with the liberation theology movement, and given the disobedience of the two priests, he communicated to the military government that Yorio and Jalics were no longer under the protection of the Catholic Church. The military took advantage of this opportunity to kidnap the two priests. In one sense, by removing protection from his Jesuit colleagues, Bergoglio left them to the mercy of the machinery of a repressive regime.

In other cases Bergoglio was accused of being closely linked with certain members of the military junta. Interestingly enough, in the book *El jesuita* the then-cardinal of Argentina agreed to speak willingly about his help and support of many priests during Videla's dictatorship. He mentioned having hidden several of them in the Society of Jesus' Máxima school:

I can't recall exactly how many, but it

was quite a few. After the death of Monsignor Enrique Angelelli (the bishop of La Rioja known for his commitment to the poor), I sheltered there in the Máximo school three seminarians from his diocese who were studying theology.[3]

In another instance Bergoglio told how he helped a young man escape with his identification card. He also advocated for several people who had been kidnapped, at least on two occasions before Videla himself and before Admiral Emilio Massera. Prior to his conversation with Videla, Jorge Mario seemingly spoke with Videla's chaplain, asking for help in persuading the general. He asked the chaplain to pretend to be sick so Bergoglio could be the one to perform mass. After mass with Videla's family, Bergoglio asked to speak with him.

Bergoglio apparently interceded for some priests who had been incarcerated and assisted in the search for a young man in the San Miguel air base.[4] He recounted to the journalist who interviewed him one of the more memorable cases:

I remember a meeting with a lady brought to me by Esther Belestrino de Careaga, the woman who, as I mentioned before, was my boss in the lab and who taught me so much about politics. She was later kidnapped and murdered and today is buried in the Santa Cruz church in Buenos Aires. This lady came from Avellaneda, in the Greater Buenos Aires area, and she had two young sons who had been married for two or three years. They had both been labeled militant communist workers and had been kidnapped. Widowed, those two boys were the only thing she had left in life. How she wept! I will never forget that image. I made a few inquiries that didn't get me anywhere, and I often rebuke myself for not having done more.[5]

Perhaps this is the main question: Did Bergoglio do enough? We could also ask ourselves, what would we have done if it meant risking our lives?

Bergoglio also related a case in which he intervened and obtained the positive result of a young man's freedom.[6] Although he tried to help different priests, he did not publicize the intervention, in spite of the accusations that he had collaborated with the dictatorship. Are these examples enough to exonerate him from what happened to his two Jesuit brothers Yorio and Jalics? As Bergoglio put it,

To answer that, I have to explain that they were working on founding a religious congregation, and they turned in the first draft of the Rules to the monsignors Pironio, Zazpes, and Serra. I still have the copy they gave me. The superior general of the Jesuits who, at that time, was Father Arrupe, said they should choose between the community where they were living and the Society of Jesus, and he ordered that they change communities. Since they stuck with their project, and the group was dissolved, they requested to leave the society. It was a long internal process that lasted more than a year. I just expedited their transfer. . . . Given the rumors of an impending coup, I warned them to be very careful. I remember I offered, in case it became necessary for their safety, that they could come live at the society's house in the province.[7]

In the first part of his answer to the complex question of the kidnapped Jesuits, Bergoglio was clearly trying to explain the situation the two priests were in and the different options they were given before they left the society. The two Jesuits rejected the options, preferring to put themselves at risk instead of abandoning their parishioners, though their actions could eventually cost them their lives. Bergoglio seemingly interceded on their behalf on two occasions after they disappeared: once before Videla and another time before Massera. Bergoglio explained,

[Yorio and Jalics] lived in what was called the Bajo Flores neighborhood of Rivadavio. I never believed they were involved in "subversive activities" as their pursuers claimed, and truly they were not. But because of their relationship with some of the priests in the slums, they became targets during the paranoia of the witch hunt. Since they lived in the neighborhood, Yorio and Jalics were kidnapped during a military sweep of the area. . . . Fortunately, they were released a short time later, first because they couldn't be accused of anything, and second, because we got on the ball and acted. The very night I learned of their kidnapping I got busy.[8]

Some accused Bergoglio of supporting the

regime's ideology and approving of the kidnapping of the priests by withdrawing the Society of Jesus' protection from them, but Bergoglio has always denied these charges. Alicia Oliveira, a criminal judge in Buenos Aires, has confirmed Bergoglio's efforts to help those kidnapped by the regime. She testified that Bergoglio came to see her about the case of someone he was trying to defend at the time:

I remember that Bergoglio came to see me about a problem with someone, sometime in 1974 or 1975, and we started talking, and we got along very well. . . . In one of our conversations we talked about the likelihood of an impending coup. He was a provincial superior of the Jesuits and surely was more informed than I was. . . . Bergoglio was very worried about what he sensed was coming. Knowing my commitment to human rights, he feared for my life. He even suggested that I come live for a while in the Máximo school. But I didn't accept. I answered with a terribly unfortunate joke given all that came to pass in the country: "I'd rather be kidnapped by the military than go live with the priests!"[9]

The Argentine Adolfo Pérez Esquivel, winner of the Nobel Peace Prize, categorically rejected the accusations against Bergoglio in a televised interview with the BBC: "Some bishops were accomplices of the Argentine dictatorship, but Bergoglio was not."[10] The proof seems convincing. Many others have testified to being protected by Bergoglio during the dictatorship.

In the face of accusations raised by media outlets about Bergoglio's collaboration with Videla, one of the kidnapped Jesuits, Father Franz Jalics, declared, "These are the facts: Orlando Yorio and I were not reported by Father Bergoglio."[11]

The 1970s military regime in Argentina represents the devastating cruelty and destruction that people can commit, even in the name of religion. Bergoglio himself condemned this widespread idea of killing in the name of religion: "Killing in the name of God is blasphemy."[12]

CHAPTER 4
THE ASCENT OF
A HUMBLE MAN

God writes my life's bestseller.[1]

Jorge Mario Bergoglio did not seem like the kind of priest who would have a dazzling ecclesiastical career. He began seminary at age twenty-one and became provincial superior at around forty. Until relatively recently, the Jesuits had remained under the rule imposed by their founder St. Ignatius of Loyola not to hold the offices of bishop, archbishop, or cardinal. When men entered the Jesuit order, they knew that the highest position to which they could aspire was superior general of the Society of Jesus. While this position is by no means insignificant, since the society has had great influence in Rome throughout history, more ambitious churchmen have generally sought simpler paths.

Jorge Mario's ecclesiastical career continued along educational pathways throughout the 1980s. From 1980 to 1986, he was the school president of the *Colegio Máximo* and the *Facultad de Filosofía y Teología* (Máximo School and the School of Philosophy and Theology), while continuing to serve as the Patriarca San José parish priest in the diocese of San Miguel. In 1986, Bergoglio left his beloved Argentina to finish his doctoral thesis in Germany. Upon his return he was sent to the *Colegio del Salvador* (School of the Savior) and later to a parish of the society in Córdoba, Argentina.

A somewhat shy man, Bergoglio simply did his job in Córdoba and expected nothing in return. Then, at the age of fifty-five, he was named bishop. While Bergoglio continued his teaching and pastoral work in Córdoba, the archbishop of Buenos Aires, Cardinal Antonio Quarracino, noticed his qualities and his modesty and decided to include Bergoglio as one of his aides.

AUXILIARY BISHOP AND ARCHBISHOP CANDIDATE

After serving the archbishop of Buenos Aires for one year, Bergoglio became his primary assistant, confirming his position as auxiliary bishop and future archbishop. Quarracino named him vicar general.

Archbishop Antonio Quarracino, of Italian origin just like Bergoglio, had had a career path similar to Jorge Mario's. He had been ordained a priest at age twenty-two and had dedicated himself to teaching, first in the diocesan seminary of Mercedes and later as a theology professor at Argentina Catholic University.

In 1962, Pope John XXIII named Quarracino bishop of Avellaneda. At that time he was closely aligned with protest movements of third-world priests, but over the years he adopted less progressive positions.

Pope John Paul II positioned Quarracino at the helm of the Catholic Church in Argentina, first promoting him to the archdiocese of La Plata and later, in 1990, to the archdiocese of Buenos Aires. After being elected president of the Argentine Episcopal Conference in 1990, Quarracino was named cardinal in 1991. He was one of the first archbishops to cultivate a relationship with Judaism. These were all steps that Bergoglio himself would later follow.

On being named bishop and in fulfillment of canonical law, each bishop must oversee a diocese. Bergoglio's first episcopal position was in the titular diocese of Auca, without territorial jurisdiction since the seventh century. Its name comes from when it was territorial and located within the

Spanish town of Villafranca Montes de Oca, a municipality in Burgos. Bergoglio held the position from 1992 to 1998. When Antonio Quarracino became ill, Bergoglio was named bishop coadjutor in 1997.

The year 1998 held profound changes for Bergoglio's life. Very few priests, and even fewer Jesuits, reach the position of archbishop. Since Bergoglio had already served Quarracino for several years, very little changed in the diocese's functionality when he became archbishop of Buenos Aires. Younger priests quickly aligned themselves with the new archbishop's vision. Bergoglio's style stood out immediately. He was simple, unpretentious, straightforward, and opposed to pomp. He continued his pastoral work among priests, even staying to take care of one who had become ill.

Being named archbishop also did little to change Bergoglio's daily routines. He continued using public transportation to maneuver through the city, and he declined the privilege of living in the luxurious archbishop's palace in the neighborhood of Olivos, very near the presidential residence. He remained very accessible, managing his own schedule and receiving anyone who came to see him.

The new archbishop avoided charity

events, galas, and the social gatherings of the aristocracy. He always dressed simply in his priest's robes. It is said that when he received word that he would be proposed for cardinal in 2001, he did not want to have new clothes tailor-made for his position. Bergoglio preferred to have the vestments of the former cardinal adapted to his size. He even declined to have a group of his parishioners accompany him to his appointment as cardinal in Rome, requesting that they instead direct to the poor the money they would have spent.

His care for the poor is legendary. In one of his frequent visits to one of Buenos Aires's slums, when he visited the parish of *Nuestra Señora de Caacupé* (Our Lady of Caacupé) in the Barracas neighborhood, a construction worker told him, "I'm proud of you, because when I was on my way back here on the bus with my friends, I saw you sitting in one of the seats at the back, just like anyone else. I told my friends, but they didn't believe me."[2] The poor felt he was just like them, and they gladly supported him when the Curia called him to serve.

Buenos Aires's current auxiliary bishop gave an interview about the new pope to the newspaper *El Tiempo:*

Monsignor, how do you know the current pope?

When he was named auxiliary bishop of Buenos Aires, I was a priest in the archdiocese. They named him archbishop, and, on Monsignor Bergoglio's recommendation, Benedict XVI named me auxiliary bishop of Buenos Aires.

Some people associate Cardinal Bergoglio with the dictator Videla and distance him from the Kirchners ever since he confronted the late former president Nestor Kirchner over the subject of homosexual marriage. Is that accurate?

There is no indication whatsoever that he was implicated in the dictatorship. Furthermore, he had no hierarchical position within the Church to even make that worth pursuing.

What do you remember of his teaching from when he was archbishop of Buenos Aires?

He always said that when you want to look at the heart, the center of something, if you start on the outskirts and go the entire way around, you will come to understand reality much better. He always talks about the great divisions and social injustices of our day. This can be a strong contribution to the Church's vision: looking from the outside in, from the periphery to the center.

Did you know him as a child?

Soon thereafter. He was studying in a secular public school. He went to the university and then entered seminary in Buenos Aires, which at that time was under Jesuit leadership. He had also felt drawn by the charisma of St. Ignatius of Loyola.[3]

Throughout his time as archbishop, Bergoglio always followed a moderate and conservative line yet also closely aligned himself with the poor. At times his criticisms of politics and the country's economic system earned him enemies, and people who were in favor of a church that was more distanced from social issues rejected his positions. In his Te Deum speech in the Cathedral of Buenos Aires on March 25, 2000, with President Francisco de la Rúa in attendance, he said,

Sometimes I wonder if we are not marching, in certain situations in the life of our society, like a sad procession; and if we do not demand to put the tombstone over this search, we are headed inexorably toward a final destination tied up in impossibilities, and we settle for small dreams bereft of hope. We must humbly recognize that the system has fallen under a broad sweep of shadow: the shadow of mistrust; and that many of the promises and declarations ring like a funeral march: everyone consoles the relatives, but no one raises the dead man.[4]

Despite Bergoglio's estranged relationship with leftist groups in the country, he called the secretary of the interior to complain when he saw police attacking the victims of the *corralito* in 2001, when banks forbade citizens from withdrawing their savings.

Argentina's political and economic situation was in chaos, and poverty was on the rise. The banks closed their doors on clients, and the political elite seemed absent, resigned to the situation. No one overlooked the fact that the archbishop of Buenos Aires was so critical of the political scene. In 2004, Bergoglio was elected president of the Argentine Episcopal Conference and reelected in 2007.

Not everyone is pleased with the new Pope Francis and the former archbishop of Buenos Aires. Many find unforgivable his pro-life stance against abortion and his opposition to homosexual marriage, an issue that estranged him from the presidential family.

Bergoglio was called upon to testify in the 2010 trial regarding human rights crimes committed in the *Escuela Superior de Mecánica de la Armada* (the Navy School of Mechanics). The archbishop testified for more than four hours regarding the arrest of the two Jesuit priests discussed earlier. He has also had to appear before the courts in a case filed by the association of the *Abuelas de la Plaza de Mayo* (Grandmothers of the Plaza de Mayo) over the appropriation of several babies by Argentine military leaders. Bergoglio was implicated in the case of Ana de la Cuadra, the stolen granddaughter of one of the founders and the first president of the association of the *Abuelas de la Plaza de Mayo.* The father of the disappeared mother, pregnant at the time of her kidnapping, had written Bergoglio asking for help. He always maintained that he had played no relevant part in the outcome of the case and that he had done what he could at the time.[5]

Jorge Mario Bergoglio's journey, from his vocational call that early spring day through illness, seminary, university, teaching career, doctoral degree, bishopric, and being named archbishop, undoubtedly formed his definite, strong character. He is tenacious yet calm, timid but direct, and above all, a defender of the poor. The influence of those around him — from his grandmother and parents to the former archbishop of Buenos Aires — fashioned Bergoglio into one of the strongest candidates to the papacy in the current-day Catholic Church. Yet how did a simple Jesuit reach the Curia of Rome? What was Bergoglio's role in the "New Evangelization" and in the Latin American Episcopal Council? What was his relationship with John Paul II? How did he take his defeat in the Conclave of 2005? What was his relationship with Benedict XVI? And, finally, how did he become the new pope? What does it mean for a Jesuit, the third pontificate so far in the twenty-first century, to be at the helm of the See of Rome?

To answer these questions we turn to the cardinal of the Jesuits.

■ ■ ■ ■

PART II
CARDINAL OF
THE JESUITS

■ ■ ■ ■

CHAPTER 5
THE JESUITS
THE POPE'S ARMY

A curious Dominican asks a Jesuit, "Is it true that Jesuits always answer one question with another question?"

"And who told Your Reverence such a thing?"

THE LIFE OF
ST. IGNATIUS OF LOYOLA

Iñigo de Loyola López de Recalde was born in 1491 in the Loyola castle in the Spanish province of Guipúzcoa. He was the youngest son of eight children, restricted to service in the military or to a religious life. When the count of Castille, Juan Velázquez de Cuellar, asked Iñigo's father to send one of his sons to become his protégé, the youngest son was chosen.

Iñigo spent at least eleven years in the city of Arévalo, making occasional trips to Villadolid with his mentor. In 1517, Velázquez fell into disgrace after the death of the Catholic King Ferdinand. Velázquez died soon after, and his widow sent Iñigo to the Duke of Nájera, Antonio Manrique de Lara, who at the time was the viceroy of Navarre.

Iñigo stood out in Navarre for his courage and determination, above all in the *Guerra de las Comunidades de Castilla* (War of the Communities of Castile) and in conflicts that arose within Guipúzcoa. Yet one event would radically change his life. French-Navarrese troops arrived in 1521 to recover the lands of Navarre. Iñigo resisted the attackers in the castle of Pamplona. In the heat of the battle, a cannonball injured both of his legs, causing Iñigo to return home to recover. In this period of enforced rest, the young man began to read, which changed his life indelibly.

Among other texts he read *Vita Christ* (*Life of Christ*) by the Carthusian Ludolph of Saxony, Jacobus de Voragine's *Legenda aurea* (*Golden Legend*), and other works on the lives of saints. Iñigo's life changed from that of the typical quarrelsome, womanizing soldier to that of a devout man pursuing holiness, as he described in his autobiography:

[A]nd when he had gained no little

spiritual light from the reading of pious books, he began to think more seriously of his past life, and how much penance he should do to expiate his past sins.

Amid these thoughts the holy wish to imitate saintly men came to his mind; his resolve was not more definite than to promise with the help of divine grace that what they had done he also would do. After his recovery his one wish was to make a pilgrimage to Jerusalem. He fasted frequently and scourged himself to satisfy the desire of penance that ruled in a soul filled with the spirit of God.[1]

The young Iñigo combined his militarism with his mysticism to form the Society of Jesus. At first he planned to travel to the Holy Land right away, but he spent roughly ten months in Manresa, Spain, assisting the work of some pious women. There he lived in a cave, meditating and fasting. That experience led him to draft the first version of his *Spiritual Exercises,* which would become the backbone of his ministry. The final book would not be published for more than twenty-six years, in 1548.

Iñigo finally decided to first visit Rome, then Jerusalem. After a brief stay in the Holy Land, he returned to the Iberian Peninsula, where he studied theology at the University of Alcalá de Henares from 1526 to 1527. However, the secret police of the Inquisition, suspicious of his teachings about self-examination and introspection, forced him to escape to Salamanca, from which he also had to flee soon after arriving.

In 1528, Iñigo ended up in Paris, where he met other Spaniards who shared his religious concerns and joined with him. These first Jesuits studied in the same classrooms as John Calvin, and a few years later became the great pursuers of the teachings of this Frenchman.

THE FOUNDING OF
THE SOCIETY OF JESUS

The founding of the Society of Jesus was plagued with setbacks, and faced with economic problems, Iñigo — who by this time had changed his name to Ignatius — raised money in Flanders and in England. Later, in a solemn act in the Church of Saint Peter of Montmartre in Paris, on the feast day of the Assumption in 1534, Ignatius and his disciples swore to "serve our Lord, leaving behind the things of the world."[2] Ignatius was forty-four years old. At that time everyone thought he was founding a mission order to evangelize in lands of unbelievers, but it would become an order of teachers and apologists, particularly active in the fight against Protestantism, which was spreading to nearly every kingdom in Europe.

The members of the Society of Jesus headed to Venice, Italy, to accompany an expedition against the Turks, but new suspicion on the part of the Inquisition once again changed Ignatius's plans. He decided it would be best to draw up a constitution for the Society of Jesus and seek official authorization from the Catholic Church for its ministry.

In 1540, Ignatius and his friends wrote the constitution, and Pope Paul III, after some hesitation, approved it. Some of the characteristics of the new order were troublesome for many people. The Society of Jesus would obey the pope alone, without being under the ecclesiastical authority of any diocese or bishop; the order would not found formal monasteries; and it would follow to the letter of the law a vow of poverty. The Jesuits also would decline any ecclesiastical appointment. They were God's marines.

In addition to the impressive missionary work the Society of Jesus carried out in Asia and the Americas, its greatest contribution to the sixteenth and seventeenth centuries was its role in the religious battle against Protestantism. The staunch defense of Catholic orthodoxy and the fact that it became the executing arm of the pope stand out clearly in the comments of the Jesuit Rouquette:

> Let us never forget that, historically, "ultramontanism" has been the practical affirmation of "universalism." . . . This necessary universalism would be an empty word if it did not result in a practical obedience or cohesion of Christianity; therefore Ignatius wanted his team to be at the pope's disposition . . . and to be the defender of Catholic unity, which is achieved only through effective submission to Christ's vicar.[3]

The papacy utilized the Jesuits to monitor the orthodoxy of Catholic monarchs and to try to woo Protestants back to the Catholic Church.

> Wherever in Europe the interests of Rome required that the populace should be stirred up against the king or that any measures of a temporal ruler which might be inconvenient to the Church

had to be countered by intrigue, propaganda and, if the occasion called for it, open rebellion, the Papal See knew full well that, for carrying out such work, there were none more reliable, more resourceful and more courageous than the fathers of the Society of Jesus.[4]

How did the Society of Jesus achieve its aims? The main instrument used was always education. They founded schools throughout the world but especially in Protestant countries. These schools were geared toward educating the elite and the nobility of each kingdom. When they managed to change their elite students' minds, it was only a matter of time before the masses would return to Catholic orthodoxy. This approach worked very well in kingdoms like Poland, Bavaria, the Rhinelands, the Saar, Hungary, and Austria. The Jesuits also entered China in 1583 and began missions in the Americas, particularly Peru and Mexico.

JESUITS IN THE FOLLOWING CENTURIES

In the following centuries, especially the seventeenth and eighteenth, when monarchies sought to accumulate more and more power and wealth even to the detriment of the Catholic Church, the Jesuits came to be perceived as enemies of the state. Absolute monarchs promoted national churches along the lines of Protestantism while Rome lost its effective power over those kingdoms. Movements such as Jansenism and Gallicanism advocated for greater independence from Rome and for limiting Rome's economic and political power. In Protestant territories the distrust of the Society of Jesus grew to such an extent that John Adams, former president of the United States, commented,

I do not like the reappearance of the Jesuits. . . . If ever there was a body of men who merited eternal damnation on earth and in hell, it is this Society of Loyola's. Nevertheless, we are compelled by our system of religious toleration to offer them an asylum.[5]

In the United States and other mainly Protestant nations, there was such a fear of the Society of Jesus that conspiracy theories began to spread, pitting it and the papacy against the United States, particularly Abraham Lincoln. A significant case in point is a supposed declaration — of which there is no official documentation or proof

— in which the questionable religious polemicist Charles Paschal Telesphore Chiniquy has Abraham Lincoln commenting on the Society of Jesus:

This war would never have been possible without the sinister influence of the Jesuits. We owe it to Popery that we now see our land reddened with the blood of her noblest sons. . . . I conceal what I know, on that subject, from the knowledge of the nation; for if the people knew the whole truth, this war would turn into a religious war, and it would, at once, take a tenfold more savage and bloody character . . . if they could hear what Professor Morse has said to me of the plots made in the very city of Rome to destroy this Republic.[6]

Some held that the Jesuits were behind the assassination of President Lincoln, and it seemed that every camp suspected the Jesuits for various conspiracies and crimes. While the majority of the widespread allegations against the Jesuits were never proved, their decline in kingdoms such as Spain was hastened by just such suspicions and a few cases of certainty.

One of the great causes for suspicion of

the Jesuits had to do with, curiously enough, the great economic power they achieved, to the point of becoming lenders and guarantors even of entire governments. This network of international loans was somewhat similar to what was developed centuries before by the order of the Templars. Bishop Palafox, whom Pope Innocent VIII had sent to the Americas, wrote to the pontiff in 1647, "I found almost all the wealth, all immovables and all treasures of this Province of America, in the hands of the Jesuits."[7]

Whether the Jesuits were falsely accused or not, the truth is Europe began to expel them: France in 1763 and then Spain and Portugal in 1767. The courts appealed to Pope Clement XIV to suppress the society completely. In 1773, Pope Clement XIV penned the *Dominus ac Redemptor,* in which he did officially suppress the Jesuits. The superior general of the Society of Jesus, Lorenzo Ricci, and his assistant counselor were jailed without trial in the Castel Sant'Angelo in Rome. Many Jesuits sought refuge in Russia, where the edict was not put into effect, and the czarina Catherine the Great gave them asylum.

THE RESTORATION OF THE JESUITS

The end of the eighteenth and beginning of the nineteenth centuries could not have been more turbulent. The French Revolution and the independence movements throughout the American continent put the Catholic Church in check, and Pope Pius VII decided to restore the Society of Jesus. The objective of the restored society would be to combat Freemasonry and liberals, which threatened to destroy the Catholic Church, especially in Europe.

Toward the end of the eighteenth century, the bishop John Carroll, a former Jesuit, founded the University of Georgetown in Washington, DC. After the restoration of the society in the nineteenth century, Georgetown would become one of the first universities to return under the influence of the Jesuits.

In Russia the Jesuits came out of asylum to reassemble the religious order. They faced several major difficulties, including the unification of Italy in 1870 and the disappearance of the Papal States. The superior general of the Jesuits escaped from Rome under pressure from the new Italian state, and the Holy See declared itself a prisoner of the same. From Fiesole, Italy, Superior General Luís Martín continued to lead the Society of Jesus.

During the first few years of the twentieth century, the superior general of the Jesuits was the German Franz Xaver Wenz, and the Jesuits numbered around fifteen thousand. The Polish Wlodimir Ledóchowski, superior general throughout World War I, reorganized and modernized the order. They suffered major setbacks when the Second Spanish Republic dissolved the Society of Jesus in 1932 and then also throughout World War II.

A Change in Jesuit Theology and Teaching

After the war the Belgian Jean-Baptiste Janssens became the superior general. Along with other Jesuit theologians, including Jean Daniélou, Henry de Lubac, and the Dominican Yves Congar, Janssens developed a new school of thought in France called the *Nouvelle Théologie* (New Theology). Thus the Jesuits transitioned from being the bastion of Catholic orthodoxy to becoming the Church's progressive vanguard.

Pope Pius XII and the Roman Curia viewed the *Nouvelle Théologie* with skepticism, as a threat to the unity and orthodoxy of the Catholic Church. In 1950, the pope condemned many of their principles in his encyclical *Humani generis.* From the 1950s on, the liberalization of the Society of Jesus worried the Holy See.

On the one hand, the Jesuit archaeologist Pierre Teilhard de Chardin was defending the theories of evolution. On the other, Jesuit theologian John Courtney Murray was defending religious liberty and interfaith dialogue. The Vatican reacted against both postures, and the Jesuit superior general ordered Teilhard to leave the academic world and sign a document withdrawing his controversial statements. In the 1960s, the expulsion of all priests from Cuba also affected the Jesuits and their schools on the island.

In 1965, Father Arrupe was elected superior general of the Society of Jesus, and he continued the social emphasis of his predecessor. At this time the future Pope Francis was finishing his education and beginning his formation as a priest and Jesuit. The Jesuits St. José María Rubio and St. Alberto Hurtado were at the forefront of the Jesuits' change in mission focus. They became the best examples of ministry directed to the "least of these."

The efforts to aid the poor and the working class solidified in the formation of unions and the use of teaching as a tool for social recognition. The Second Vatican Council and the triumph of some of the positions of this sector of Jesuits, such as Murray's theories of religious freedom, put the order once again in the center of the Catholic Church's mission work. Another Jesuit theologian, Karl Rahner, developed a pastoral theology that highly valued the laity as "anonymous Christians."

After the Second Vatican Council, the Catholic Church witnessed the greatest number of priests who left their positions, many of them deciding to serve as married ministers or work in secular jobs. The Jesuits also experienced a sharp decline in numbers as around eight thousand priests left the order.

THE DECAPITATION OF THE JESUITS

Pope Paul VI tried to defend the Society of Jesus, but many dioceses were raising criticisms. The pope asked the Jesuits to submit to diocesan authority, which broke the fourth vow and the heart of the order. The new Pope John Paul II took advantage of the illness of the order's superior general, Father Arrupe, to take control of the Jesuits and halt the liberation theology that had spread so rapidly throughout the order. Calling it an extraordinary measure, John

Paul II named a pontifical delegate and a deputy to govern the order, bypassing the mechanisms to elect a new superior general. The Society of Jesus accepted the pope's decision, though many criticized this anomaly.

In 1983, the Jesuit General Congregation met and elected the Dutch Peter Hans Kolvenbach as the twenty-ninth superior general of the Society of Jesus. Kolvenbach changed the Society of Jesus' orientation, limiting the influence of their educational ministry and focusing more on refugees and immigrants.

In the 1980s and 1990s, several Jesuits were assassinated for their defense of the poor in different countries in Latin America, including Father James F. Carney in Honduras in 1983, and Ignacio Ellacuría and five other Jesuit priests in El Salvador. Assassinations of Jesuit priests also occurred in Africa, India, and Southeast Asia.

Pressure from the Curia, particularly in the more conservative papacies of John Paul II and Benedict XVI, has greatly affected the Society of Jesus in recent years. The Vatican demanded the resignation of Thomas Reese, Jesuit editor of the weekly Catholic magazine *America*. In 2007, the Holy See also condemned the work of

Spanish Jesuit theologian Jon Sobrino in El Salvador. In the two most recent papacies, the Roman Curia has leaned more heavily on conservative sectors such as Opus Dei and the Legion of Christ. At the beginning of the twenty-first century, Jesuit numbers continued to decline to just over twenty thousand, the majority of which come from Latin America, Africa, and India.

CAN A JESUIT BE POPE?

So how does the election of a priest of Jesuit origin to the papacy affect the Catholic Church? Does it indicate a swing to the left for the Roman Curia? Is it common for a Jesuit to assume such important ecclesial duties? Several voices have raised these questions, even among Jesuits themselves. According to the rules of the Society of Jesus, any member who is named bishop ceases to be under the order's jurisdiction.

Inaxio Arregi, Jesuit priest and former news director of Vatican Radio, declared that when the current pope accepted the position of bishop, he ceased to belong to the Jesuit order:

I do not think that Bergoglio is depending now nor will he depend in the future on the Jesuits. You have to remember that when a Jesuit becomes bishop, he stops depending on the Jesuit superiors and answers directly to the hierarchy of the Universal Church.[8]

Other Jesuits seem very content with the election of the new pope. Jesuit priest James Martin, author of the book *The Jesuit Guide to (Almost) Everything,* wrote for CNN about the improbability of a Jesuit becoming pope:

First, most cardinals come from the ranks of the diocesan clergy. That is, most study in diocesan seminaries and are trained to work in the more familiar Catholic settings of parishes — celebrating Masses, baptizing children, presiding at marriages and working closely with families in their parish. Their lives are perhaps more easily understood by the public at large. They begin as parish priests, and later are appointed bishops and archbishops and, later, are named cardinals by the pope.[9]

Jesuits are a minority order within the Catholic Church, and by a simple matter of statistics, it is very rare for a pope to come from a religious order. But the second reason for the surprise papal appointment of a Jesuit that James Martin offered is even more convincing:

Also, the Jesuits were sometimes viewed with suspicion in a few quarters of the Vatican. There are a number of reasons for that, some of them complex. The first is, as I mentioned, our "differentness." Second, our work with the poor and people on the margins sometimes struck some as too experimental, radical and even dangerous. "When you work on the margins," an old Jesuit said, "you sometimes step out of bounds."[10]

Perhaps the most important question of all is, how did Jorge Mario Bergoglio become a candidate for the papacy in the first place?

CHAPTER 6
SUPPORTING JOHN PAUL II IN HIS AMERICAN MINISTRY

Patiently, with paternal pedagogy, with an ever-catechizing goal, through mission work among the populace and other means of ministry, help these believers mature in their awareness of belonging to the Church and to discover the Church as their family, their home, the privileged place of their encounter with God. It is precisely these multitudes that maintain the faith of their baptism, yet probably weakened by an ignorance of religious truths and by a certain ecclesial "marginality," they are the most vulnerable to the war of secularism and the proselytism of sects. . . . The presence of these sects, acting especially over these baptized followers who have been insufficiently evangelized or distanced from sacramental practice but who have religious questions, is for us a pastoral challenge to which we must respond with a renewed missionary dynamism.[1]

John Paul II, a Polish priest who had survived the harsh communist repression in his country, made it his main goal to protect Catholics in communist nations. In his visit to Nicaragua, he chastised the priest Ernesto Cardenal for holding a position in the communist-leaning Sandinista government.

Pope John Paul II's tireless fight to protect the persecuted church earned him an assassination attempt that nearly cost him his life. It also influenced his staunch opposition to liberation theology, lead partly by the Society of Jesus in Latin America.

His closest aide for theological matters and the control of unruly members of the Catholic Church in Latin America was Joseph Ratzinger, who would succeed him as pope and who, in the 1980s, led the Congregation for the Doctrine of the Faith. Ratzinger forbade several Catholic theologians from teaching, including Leonard Boff, one of the most important proponents of liberation theology. He also halted the work of Hans Küng because of its liberalism and laxity in doctrine. Once liberation theology seemed a thing of the past and the Jesuits began to toe the line drawn for them by

John Paul II, the pope concentrated on the other open front: Protestantism in Latin America.

LATIN AMERICA: HEART OF THE CATHOLIC CHURCH

The papacy of John Paul II focused on the Americas in a special way. Of the 128 countries he visited throughout his pontificate, the majority were in Europe and the Americas. The only territories not visited by the pope on the American continent were the Guayana region and a few small Caribbean islands. All the other countries received one or more visits from him.

He visited the United States most frequently to support the Catholic community there. Four times he went to Brazil, the country with the greatest number of Catholics in Latin America and the country that loses the most followers to Protestantism.

The Catholic Church, in the Special Assembly for America of the Synod of Bishops in 1997, concluded,

A general consensus exists in all America on the serious problem posed by the religious movements and the sects, given their religious extremism and programs of proselytism. So extensive is their growth, that in the Central, South and Caribbean parts of the American hemisphere, the term "invasion" is used, in reference to the fact that many of these groups originate in the United States of America where they have abundant economic resources for the development of their campaigns. Furthermore, mention is made of the existence of a coordinated plan of all the sects to alter the present religious identity of Latin America, which, as the introduction to this document states, is essentially not only Christian but Catholic. In general, the religious movements and sects aggressively preach against the Catholic Church. Moreover, they direct their campaigns of proselytism towards the marginalized of society, immigrants, prisoners, the sick in hospitals and generally towards all who live on the periphery of the big cities, where the presence of the Catholic Church sometimes is not very strong. Some propagators of the sects interpret the Bible in a fundamentalist way, providing pat answers to people who find themselves in situations of great uncertainty. They organize groups for the study of the Bible, give speeches in town-squares and invite people to frequent the sect's places of cult. In general, the sects appeal to people's emotions and superficial sensitivities in order to develop their propaganda activities. In many groups coordinated by these movements, the physical cure of the sick is prayed for and alms are distributed to attract people. Lured by these tactics, many Catholics in recent years have abandoned the practice of their faith to enter the religious movements and the sects.[2]

The Catholic Church's concern over the spread of Protestant groups had not waned. Therefore, John Paul II chose various American bishops and priests in his confidence to help carry out his New Evangelization, though the plan was not enacted until the pontificate of Benedict XVI.

BERGOGLIO'S RISING PROFILE

The relationship between John Paul II and Jorge Mario Bergoglio began when the pope named the Argentine second auxiliary bishop of Buenos Aires. Pope John Paul II visited Argentina on two occasions, the first in 1982, when the country was in the final throes of Videla's dictatorial nightmare. At that time Bergoglio was the president of the

Máximo school of the Jesuits and had the opportunity to see the pope at some point during his stay. John Paul II visited Argentina again in 1987.

Bergoglio's ordination as cardinal on February 21, 2001, may have been the first personal encounter between the two, though they may have met at the Special Assembly for America of the Synod of Bishops in 1997, in Vatican City. It is also possible that they didn't meet until the Special Assembly in November 2004.

After being named archbishop and later as a cardinal, Bergoglio belonged to several congregations of the Curia, which required him to visit Rome more frequently. He belonged to the Sacred Congregation for the Clergy, which oversees priests who do not belong to a religious order. He was also a member of the Pontifical Council for the Family and the Congregation for Divine Worship and the Discipline of the Sacraments, which oversees the liturgy of the Catholic Church and rituals of the sacraments.

Bergoglio served as well on the Ordinary Council of the General Secretariat of the Synod of Bishops, in charge of organizing the synods or meetings of bishops. He also belonged to the Congregation for Institutes of Consecrated Life and Societies of Apostolic Life, which supervises matters related to both religious orders and congregations, and the Latin American Episcopal Conference, which outlines the policies for the Catholic Church in Latin America.

The recently named Cardinal Bergoglio caught the Curia's attention in 2001, when the archbishop of New York, who was presiding over the worldwide Synod of Bishops, had to return to the United States urgently after the September 11 attacks on the Twin Towers. In that 2001 meeting before 252 synodal fathers from 118 countries, Bergoglio, though unknown until that moment, was recognized as the general reporter. As result of his brilliant performance, he was named a member of the post-synod council, representing the American continent. In this way Bergoglio made his first international mark.

The archbishop of Buenos Aires was recognized a second time when, two years after the Conclave of 2005, in celebration of the Fifth General Conference of the Latin American and Caribbean Episcopate (known in Spanish as CELAM) in Aparecida, Brazil, he was chosen to lead the team drafting the final document, known as the "Aparecida Document."[3] This landmark conference was every bit as significant as the previous CELAM conferences in Medellín, Colombia, in 1969, and in Puebla, Mexico, in 1979.

Bergoglio's success in this conference was evident by the applause he received after officiating mass and giving his homily. None of the other participants were as celebrated as the archbishop of Buenos Aires.

The once young, timid Argentine had risen strikingly in the past few years and had now become one of the most well-known and respected men in the hierarchy of the Catholic Church. How much of the young Jesuit remained inside Cardinal Bergoglio? Would the controversial Argentine be a good candidate for the papacy? How did Cardinal Bergoglio differ from John Paul II and Pope Benedict XVI on matters of doctrine? Would it be possible for the Vatican State, closed off in a world of intrigue and influence, to elect someone with a Jesuit background, someone overtly critical of Rome's ostentatious luxury?

The first round is about to begin. But the archbishop of Buenos Aires is a hard fighter to knock down; he gets up from the mat over and over until his strength gives out completely.

CHAPTER 7
THE POTENTIAL POPE
WHO CEDED TO THE
GERMAN CANDIDATE

"What were you feeling when you heard your name over and over again in the Sistine Chapel during the scrutiny for the election of John Paul II's successor?"

Bergoglio got serious, a bit tense. Finally he smiled and said, "At the beginning of the conclave, we cardinals are sworn to secrecy; we cannot talk about what happens there."[1]

Very few humans have ever attended one of these meetings — one of the most secretive in the entire world. The conclaves have become a spectacle of increasing intrigue to mass media and the public at large. The Catholic Church itself, hoping for a bit of positive press after all the bad news surrounding the Church, sees the papal election as a way to catch the world's eye for a few days. There is no other event followed as closely worldwide as a conclave, not even the election of the president of the United States of America.

THE CONCLAVE

Merriam-Webster's defines *conclave* as "a private meeting or secret assembly; *especially:* a meeting of Roman Catholic cardinals secluded continuously while choosing a pope."[2] Yet a conclave is much more than this short definition allows.

The term *conclave* derives from the Latin *cum clavis* and literally means "with key," or "locked up." It is similar to today's colloquial phrase *behind closed doors.* Since the beginning of the Catholic Church, the conclaves have grown increasingly more reserved and secret.

Though in modern times papal influence over national governments is very limited, at other points in history, the pope could use the threat of excommunication to influence decisive political changes.

The system of requiring the papal electors to close themselves off and remain isolated from the outside world stems from the Second Council of Lyon in 1274, though the election of "Peter's successor" dates from much further back.

The conclaves have been held in Vatican

City for centuries. None other than the Sistine Chapel, arguably the most beautiful chapel in the world, is the designated setting for these ostentatious, colorful gatherings. The Sistine Chapel is part of the Apostolic Palace and dates back to 1447–80, when it was built by order of Pope Sixtus IX. Between 1508 and 1512, Pope Julius II commissioned the incredible frescoes, masterpieces of Michelangelo. Among the more famous are *The Last Judgment* and the fresco on the ceiling, *The Creation of Adam.*

Other iconic elements of the Sistine Chapel and the conclave's voting system are the chimney and the stove, where the ballots are burned. If *fumata nera,* "black smoke," arises, it means that no candidate has received enough votes to be named pope; if *fumata bianca* rises, the election is complete, and the next pope of the Catholic Church has been named.

Before the East-West Schism (the definitive break between the Latin and Greek churches, a division that still separates Roman Catholics and Eastern Orthodox), the conclaves were originally held at the Dominican Basilica Santa Maria sopra Minerva, but after 1455, they were held in the Vatican and, since 1878, have been within the Sistine Chapel. Oddly enough the Dominican Basilica Santa Maria sopra Minerva was built over the ruins of an ancient Roman temple to Minerva, goddess of wisdom, as if the cardinals were seeking the wisdom of a pagan goddess in electing their pope.

THE EVOLUTION OF THE PAPAL ELECTORAL SYSTEM

At first the election of the bishop of Rome was subject to the direct vote of the parishioners. Over time the clergy, laity, and bishops of neighboring dioceses began to intervene.

Roman tradition held that a cleric would nominate a papal candidate by consensus or acclamation and would then present the candidate before the citizens of Rome for ratification. This system had plenty of complications, given that at times the masses would elect more than one pope, resulting in the famous antipopes.

The Lateran Council of 769 abolished the right of the people of Rome to elect their bishop, but the Synod of Rome restored this right in 862, limiting it to the nobility. In 1059, Pope Nicholas II introduced a change that assured the decision would remain in the hands of the Church. He ordered the election of the pope to be the responsibility of the cardinals, subject to ratification by the Roman laity and clergy. The Lateran Council of 1139 introduced a final change, eliminating the need for ratification and thus creating the current system of papal election. This system has been questioned only once, during the East-West Schism.

The cloistering of the electors became necessary due to the strong influence secular rulers exercised over their cardinals. At times conclaves seemed to last forever, blocked by electors who wanted to hinder the election of a certain pope. Despite the request to be cloistered, some cardinals would leave the conclave, and at times only force would keep them in attendance. The conclave after the death of Pope Clement IV (1268) was one of the longest, requiring the cardinals to remain within the Apostolic Palace for three years. The cardinals were finally relegated to a diet of bread and water until they elected a pope.

Despite these anecdotes, the majority of conclaves have been quick and uneventful. For centuries the Church has attempted to make the cardinals' stay in the Vatican more comfortable and the electoral system more regulated and efficient.

Pope Pius X gathered all the pertinent

papal norms into a constitution. In 1945, Pius XII changed a few regulations, as did Juan XXIII in 1962 and Paul VI in 1975. Pope John Paul II ordered the *Universi Dominici Gregis* in 1996, outlining the final rules of current conclaves.

ELECTIONS AND CANDIDATES

The current electors are all the members of the College of Cardinals. Though in the thirteenth century only seven cardinals voted, currently all 183 cardinals in the college vote. At one time there were only seventy cardinals, but the growth and spread of the Catholic Church obligated Pope John XXIII to increase the number of cardinals to adequately represent the greater number of countries with Catholic presence. In 1970, Pope Paul VI capped the election age to eighty years, meaning that only candidates younger than eighty can vote.

Any baptized Catholic can become a candidate to the papacy; being clergy is not a requirement. During the eighth century papal candidacy was limited first to all clergy and eventually to only cardinals. This norm was overturned in the Third Lateran Council in 1179, opening the papacy back up to any believing Catholic male.

In case the Catholic Church elected a lay-man or a mere priest as pope, after having accepted the responsibility, this man would have been named a bishop. Yet candidates had to fulfill at least two canonical regulations to be named bishop: being over thirty-five years of age and having served at least five years as a priest.

Though the majority of popes elected by the Catholic Church have been Italian, papal candidates can be from any country and race but never female. Until the election of John Paul II, Italian popes had dominated the role for nearly five hundred years. The tendency now seems to internationalize the position, given that John Paul II's successor was the German Benedict XVI and the current Pope Francis is Argentine.

ELECTORAL PROCEEDINGS AND THE POPE'S PROCESS OF TAKING OFFICE

Unlike modern political elections, a papal election does not involve the rivalry of two or more candidates. Cardinals cannot offer themselves as candidates nor campaign to their own advantage. They are allowed to discuss the best candidates and to support third parties.

Throughout history the election of the

pope has occurred in three different ways: by acclamation, compromise, or scrutiny. In acclamation, the electors simply name aloud, or acclaim, the one they elect, as if inspired by the Holy Spirit, and if the vote is unanimous, then he is automatically elected pope. Election by compromise has been used in difficult moments when the cardinals have been unable to come to agreement. In this case, a commission of cardinals is chosen to elect the pope. The most common method, and the only one allowed since Pope John Paul II issued the *Universi Dominici Gregis* in 1996, is scrutiny, using secret ballots.

Popes were elected originally by simple majority, but the Third Lateran Council increased the percentage to a two-thirds majority vote. Cardinals are not allowed to vote for themselves. If, after thirty-four rounds of voting, a pope has not been elected, a simple majority is accepted. During his pontificate, Benedict XVI reinstated the requisite majority to two-thirds plus one, to preclude a papacy in constant dispute.

When the see of the bishop of Rome or the pope becomes vacant, *sede vacante* in Latin, the first few words of the Apostolic Constitution *Universi Dominici Gregis* are pronounced. The Latin phrase utilized means "Shepherd of the Lord's entire flock." The Holy See typically becomes vacant for one of two reasons: the pope either dies or resigns. A third reason would be the deposition of a pope, but this is not included in the norms of the Vatican.

It is very rare for a pope to resign from his position. When it happens, the constitution requires a free and formal election. The next chapter will discuss what led to Pope Benedict XVI's resignation.

When a pope is hindered from fulfilling his duties due to outside forces, such as capture, banishment, exile, or disability, it is called *sede impedite* in Latin.

During the election of the new pope and while the see remains vacant, the College of Cardinals assumes the government of the Catholic Church, with limited responsibilities. They can make decisions regarding only commonplace, unavoidable issues. They are also responsible for organizing the pope's funeral and the election of his successor. The College of Cardinals cannot change the election rules or turn into a papal substitute.

During the period of a *sede vacante,* the cardinal camerlengo takes charge of the papal assets, assisted by three other cardinals. Since 2007 the cardinal camerlengo has been Tacisio Bertone, who also serves as the secretary of state of the Vatican.

THE START OF THE CONCLAVE

At the beginning of the conclave, the cardinals gather in Rome and enter Vatican City, staying in the Casa Santa Maria, which Pope John Paul II outfitted for the comfort of the electors. The residence is within the Vatican itself and is near the Sistine Chapel.

Throughout the days or weeks that a conclave might last, all communication with the outside world is prohibited, including television, telephone, radio, Internet, or any form of correspondence. The electors are isolated to safeguard the cardinals from outside influence and to assure the freedom of their decision and the seclusion necessary for casting such an important vote.

Conclaves tend to begin fifteen to twenty days after the death or resignation of a pope. The inaugural ceremony is held in the morning in a solemn votive mass called the *Pro eligendo Summo Pontifice,* presided over by the cardinal dean. In this celebration they ask God to enlighten the cardinals in the election of the new pope.

In the afternoon all the cardinals gathered in the Pauline Chapel proceed to the Sistine Chapel. They pass through the Sala Regia, where in earlier times the pope sat enthroned. Once arranged and having sung the *Veni Creator,* they take the oaths, the doors of the Sistine Chapel are shut, and only the cardinals remain, with Swiss guards standing at the door to protect the electoral process.

There are two sessions per day, one in the morning and one in the afternoon, with two rounds of voting each. The electors each receive two ballots with the words *Eligo in Summum Pontificem,* "I elect as Supreme Pontiff," followed by a blank space where they can write the name of a candidate. The cardinals are asked to write legibly yet without a recognizable hand.

The cardinals fold up their ballots and take them to the altar, where the scrutineers receive them in a covered container. As each cardinal approaches the ballot box, he says, "I call as my witness Christ the Lord who will be my judge, that my vote is given to the one who before God I think should be elected." If a cardinal is too old or sick to walk forward, the scrutineer goes to collect his ballot and take it to the ballot box. If the cardinal is on bed rest, the scrutineers go to his room to collect his ballot.

Three cardinal scrutineers, chosen by lot,

count the ballots before everyone. If there are more votes than electors, all ballots are burned and the process begins again. Three revisers check the scrutineers' count. The ballots are then burned in a chimney, changing the color of smoke according to whether the election was conclusive or not. The elections are registered in a special record.

PROCLAMATION OF THE POPE

When the necessary majority has been reached, the secretary of the College of Cardinals and the master of Papal Liturgical Celebration return to the Sistine Chapel. The cardinal dean approaches the papal candidate and asks, *"Acceptasne electionem de te canonice factam in Summum Pontificem?"* ("Do you accept your canonical election as supreme pontiff?"). If the candidate accepts, he is asked, *"Quo nomine vis vocari?"* ("By what name do you wish to be called?"). The new pope then announces his new name, saying, *"Vocabor . . ."* ("I am called . . ."). The master of celebration makes note of the name of the new pope in the official record.

THE CONCLAVES OF 1978

The last few conclaves have been very different. The final conclave of the twentieth century, which led to the pontificate of John Paul II, broke with tradition. A non-Italian pope had not been elected since the sixteenth century, and when the conclave was convened in 1978, there was not yet a clear candidate.

The proclamation of the pope had been nearly instant: after one day and only four rounds of voting, the patriarch of Venice, Albino Luciani, became the new pope. Yet his death was as sudden as his rise to the pontificate. The pope had assumed his responsibilities just a short time before, in August 1978. After holding the position for only thirty-three days, he was found dead in his bed.

The sudden death of John Paul I left the Catholic Church in a state of confusion. The Church deemed it best to replace him immediately, and a new conclave was convened that same year, in October 1978.

The election of a pope with Polish background demonstrated the Catholic Church's interest in focusing on the suffering of its followers in communist countries, but John Paul II's pontificate accomplished much more. The young Polish pope carried out some of the plans of his predecessor. He also brought the papacy into the center of attention for both the media and the world's interested public. As previously mentioned, he made countless trips throughout his twenty-seven years as pope. He altered the Vatican's approach toward common people while remaining faithful to Catholic tradition in matters of doctrine and liturgy. The Polish pope attempted to unite the church and do away with politicizing trends like liberation theology. Toward these ends he relied heavily on more conservative sectors, such as Opus Dei and the Legion of Christ. His friend and coworker Joseph Aloisius Ratzinger was groomed to continue the work of his predecessor.

THE CONCLAVE OF 2005

The first conclave of the twenty-first century was a highly anticipated event. The world looked on with keen interest as the health of the strong, active John Paul II deteriorated to unexpected degrees. Some advised him to resign, but he held to his position, convinced that the only way to abandon the pontificate was through death.

John Paul II was eighty-four years old when he died on April 2, 2005. His charisma had won over even many of his opponents. His polemical visits, with a clear political intention yet driven by his desire to support Catholics wherever they were, had won him great respect. Who could replace a man of such stature?

The last words of the Polish Pope John Paul II were, *"Pozwólcie mi iść do domu Ojca"* ("Let me go to the house of the Father").[3] Right away the crowds clamored for his beatification, and his remains were eventually placed in the altar in the Chapel of St. Sebastian.

On April 8, 2005, the state funeral for Pope John Paul II began. An estimated 300,000 people fit into St. Peter's Square for the occasion, but there were over 1.5 million pilgrims gathered in Vatican City. The leaders of the world's most powerful countries represented their nations at the funeral, and all ecclesial positions were represented. There among the crowd of cardinals, a man from Argentina, Jorge Mario Bergoglio, grieved the death of his superior, completely unaware of what would occur in only a few days.

The conclave began just ten days later, on April 18, 2005. Expectations were extremely high. It was difficult to find a suitable replacement after a papacy as long as John Paul II's. One of the first decisions made by the College of Cardinals was that the candidate should not be older than eighty years of age. They did not want to repeat the agonizing last few years of the previous pope.

There were 117 cardinals eligible for the conclave at that time. The majority were European, with fifty cardinals. Eighteen were from North America and seventeen from Latin America, with the rest spread throughout Africa, Asia, and Oceania. For health reasons, Cardinals Jaime Lachica Sin and Adolfo Antonio Suárez Rivera were unable to attend.

Among the Latin Americans, Monsignor Jorge Mario Bergoglio represented Argentina. Although well known to the Curia by this point, he was a complete stranger to Catholics at large and the media.

THE DERAILED ELECTION OF JORGE MARIO BERGOGLIO

The first day of the conclave included the rites as described above. After the long pontificate of John Paul II, only two cardinals present had participated in the previous conclave, Cardinal Baum and Ratzinger himself.

There were two somewhat unique cardinals at the conclave, Ignatius Basile Moses I Daoud, of the Syrian Catholic Church, and Lubomyr Husar, of the Ukranian Catholic Church. The rest belonged to the Roman Catholic Church.

The master of Papal Liturgical Celebration at the time was Piero Marini. In the first debate no majority was reached, though everyone knew that Ratzinger, John Paul II's right hand for so many years, was the favorite.

The octogenarian Cardinal Spidlik led the afternoon meditation. After a brief homily the cardinals approached the altar in order to cast their votes. Whom did they have in mind? Who could possibly replace the most charismatic pope of the last few centuries?

The cardinals who received votes were Ratzinger with forty-seven votes, Bergoglio with ten, Carlo Martini with nine, Camillo Ruini with six, Angelo Sodano with four, Óscar Rodríguez Maradiaga with three, and Dionigi Tettamanzi with the remaining two votes. The front-runner, Ratzinger, had been the pope's right-hand man; he was also the dean of the College of Cardinals and the candidate best situated within the Curia.

The Argentine Jorge Mario Bergoglio was a surprise to most cardinals, though he had become better known in the past few years, especially in the American continent.

Given his vast academic training, Cardinal Martini had been one of the favorites in the conclave, yet some thought that at seventy-eight he was too close to the papal candidacy age limit. He had been the archbishop of Milan for twenty years. Martini was the most progressive candidate within the Catholic Church at that time.

The rest of the candidates seemed to have very little chance of actually becoming pope, but the talk among the cardinals that day was the surprising candidacy of their Argentine colleague.

At mealtime and in the rest of the meetings, Bergoglio remained aloof, overwhelmed at the responsibility that might fall on his shoulders. The cardinal was unfamiliar with the ways of the Curia; he had never lived in Rome and had no sway with the different factions at play in the heart of the Catholic Church.

The cardinals knew that Bergoglio could be a radical. Since being named cardinal he had waved off the privilege of living in the archbishop's palace in one of the wealthiest residential areas of Buenos Aires. Some saw in him the figure of Pope John Paul I, who had been very austere in his pontificate, but others foresaw the dangers of a future pope biased toward the poor.

On Tuesday, April 19, at 9:00 a.m., the conclave gathered again. The morning's first voting session defined the positions and focused on the stronger candidates. This scrutiny resulted in sixty-five votes for Ratzinger, but he still lacked twelve to achieve the two-thirds majority. The big surprise was again Bergoglio, who earned thirty-five votes. The votes for Ruini had gone to Ratzinger, but the votes of the progressive Martini were channeled to Bergoglio. Sodano had only four votes, and Tettamanzi again garnered two.

The second day of voting seemed to be even more complex. Would more votes be directed toward the archbishop of Buenos Aires? Bergoglio commented years later that he had felt overwhelmed and embarrassed by the situation:

"What were you feeling when you heard your name over and over again in the Sistine Chapel during the scrutiny for the election of John Paul II's successor?"

Bergoglio got serious, a bit tense. Finally he smiled and said, "At the beginning of the conclave, we cardinals are sworn to secrecy, we cannot talk about what happens there."

"But you could at least tell us what you were feeling when you saw yourself among the great candidates for the papacy . . ."

"Shy, embarrassed. I thought all the journalists were crazy."[4]

The day's second session of voting was held at 11:00 a.m., and some already considered Bergoglio the future pope, to the great surprise of thousands of journalists and the millions of awaiting Catholics. Ratzinger obtained seventy-two votes in that round, still lacking five to become pope. Bergoglio's ballots increased to forty, five more than last time, which only complicated the scene.

All the cardinals were taken aback by the sudden rise of the Argentine cardinal. Bergoglio's vote count required that the cardinals go through another round. Ratzinger's supporters were surprised, having expected the German to be elected unopposed.

Lunch that day must have been lively. Many cardinals must have eyed Bergoglio to discern if this good-natured yet shy man was capable of leading the world's oldest religious organization, especially with little knowledge of the Curia's inner workings.

Cardinal Trujillo campaigned in Ratzinger's favor. Martini tried to tip the balance toward Bergoglio, encouraging the Latin American cardinals to change their votes. If they could keep the afternoon voting session inconclusive, Bergoglio could continue gathering votes the following day.

Seemingly, however, Bergoglio himself asked those voting for him to choose Ratzinger. Thus the unknown archbishop of Buenos Aires simply remained close to becoming the first Latin American pope in history.

The third voting session of that day and the fourth of the entire conclave was definite. Ratzinger achieved eighty-four votes and Bergoglio twenty-six. After the results of the scrutiny, the room was silent for a few moments before a cordial applause honored the new pope. The question then became, who was this German cardinal? Would he be able to bear the church up after John Paul II?

THE GERMAN POPE

Joseph Aloisius Ratzinger was always a studious, solitary, uncharismatic man who avoided crowds. Born in Marktl, in Baveria, he was the third and youngest child of Joseph Ratzinger, a policeman, and Maria Rieger. The young Ratzinger had always wanted to become a bishop. As a child he had seen the cardinal archbishop of Munich in a solemn ceremony and known that he wanted to become like him. He studied in the Saint Michael Seminary with his parents' support. After Hitler ordered all seminarians to join the Hitler Youth in 1939, young Ratzinger was conscripted. At sixteen he was called to serve in the army as an assistant in the anti-aircraft corps. The young soldier had to protect the BMW factory in Munich. He was later sent to Austria to work on anti-tank defenses.

The young German deserted his post in the final days of the war and was imprisoned by the Allies. After being freed he finished high school. He went on to study at the Higher School of Philosophy and Theology of Freising, the University of Munich, and the University of Freiburg. After obtaining his doctorate he began teaching at the University of Bonn in 1959. By the time he transferred to the University of Münster in 1963, he was already recognized as an important theologian.

At first Ratzinger was captivated by the *Nouvelle Théologie,* which as previously discussed was driven by the Jesuits, but little by little he drifted toward more moderate positions.

In 1966, he began teaching theology at the University of Tübingen, becoming a colleague of the famous theologian Hans

Küng. His innovative positions were already evident in his first book, *Introduction to Christianity,* in which he argued that the pope should make decisions taking into account the opinions of others. After teaching in various positions and participating in the Second Vatican Council, Ratzinger was ordained archbishop of Munich and Freising. His childhood dream had come true. Could he aspire to anything higher than German archbishop?

The arrival of John Paul II to the pontificate indicated a generational renewal. The pope ordained Ratzinger as archbishop in 1977, and the two met for the first time after years of corresponding.

John Paul II utilized the German archbishop as his closest assistant in theological matters. In 1981, Ratzinger was named prefect for the Congregation for the Doctrine of the Faith, the modern-day Inquisition. To fulfill his new responsibilities, he left the archbishopric of Germany and moved to Rome. He was later (1993) named cardinal bishop of Velletri-Segni and elected vice-dean of the College of Cardinals in 1998, becoming its dean in 2002.

Ratzinger was without a doubt the candidate better positioned to occupy Peter's seat. The German cardinal considered himself to be John Paul II's successor because they had worked so closely together. He commented,

> In this network of witnesses, the Successor of Peter has a special task. It was Peter who, on the Apostles' behalf, made the first profession of faith: "You are the Messiah, the Son of the living God" (Matt 16:16).
>
> This is the task of all Peter's Successors: to be the guide in the profession of faith in Christ, Son of the living God. The Chair of Rome is above all the Seat of this belief. . . .
>
> The Bishop of Rome sits upon the Chair to bear witness to Christ. Thus, the Chair is the symbol of the *potestas docendi,* the power to teach that is an essential part of the mandate of binding and loosing which the Lord conferred on Peter, and after him, on the Twelve.[5]

The German pope, who chose the name Benedict XVI, saw himself as continuing not only the work of St. Peter but also that of Peter's successors, especially that of his mentor, John Paul II.

It was not easy for Ratzinger to convince himself he could hold an office as complex and important as the pontificate. Hours before his election, Ratzinger's prayer was very clear:

When, little by little, the trend of the voting led me to understand that, to say it simply, the axe was going to fall on me, my head began to spin. I was convinced that I had already carried out my life's work and could look forward to ending my days peacefully. With profound conviction I said to the Lord: Do not do this to me! You have younger and better people at your disposal, who can face this great responsibility with greater dynamism and greater strength.[6]

Some cardinals held reservations about the new pope. They believed the Catholic Church needed a more dynamic, charismatic man. For this reason some thought there should have been another round of voting. Yet more than any other party, the press seemed disappointed: "Ratzinger seemed too old, too sick, too European, too intellectual, too 'hard line.' "[7]

Chapter 8
The Conclave of 2013

For this reason, and well aware of the seriousness of this act, with full freedom I declare that I renounce the ministry of Bishop of Rome, Successor of Saint Peter, entrusted to me by the Cardinals on 19 April 2005, in such a way that as from 28 February 2013, at 20:00 hours, the See of Rome, the See of Saint Peter, will be vacant and a Conclave to elect the new Supreme Pontiff will have to be convoked by those whose competence it is.[1]

Pope Benedict XVI's pontificate began April 19, 2005. He named himself after a pope who served during an extremely difficult time, elected in the middle of World War I. That pope, Benedict XV, had to fight to maintain the neutrality of the Catholic Church throughout the conflict.

Benedict XVI had served in the papal court for many years. He arrived in 1982, when John Paul II called him to serve as cardinal and prefect of the Congregation for the Doctrine of the Faith. His position as prefect had brought him many problems. The entire progressive wing of the Catholic Church saw him as a harsh conservative who defended the values of the most traditional sector. The men of Opus Dei and other conservative groups moved freely about the halls of the Vatican, yet from the start of his pontificate, these were the least of his problems.

During his tenure, Benedict XVI created new cardinalships and promoted the New Evangelization, as touched on in previous chapters. As an intellectual and theologian, he concentrated on writing books and encyclicals in an attempt to show that the Chair of St. Peter should be focused primarily on teaching. In his encyclicals he dealt with subjects such as the God of love, hope, and, especially after the onset of the economic crisis, financial difficulties. Among his most important works were his studies on the life of Jesus. The first was called *Jesus of Nazareth,* followed by *Jesus of Nazareth: Holy Week.* The third and final in the series was *Jesus of Nazareth: The Infancy Narratives,* published in 2012. Despite his positive qualities as a thinker and writer, the new pope lacked the charisma of his predecessor, and health problems hindered him from imparting the vitality needed by a new pontificate.

Pope Benedict XVI was ever under the shadow of John Paul II, though he viewed the situation as more of a blessing than a weakness. Regarding the previous pope he said, "I seem to feel his strong hand clasping mine; I seem to see his smiling eyes and hear his words, at this moment addressed specifically to me, 'Do not be afraid!' "[2] His pontificate grew increasingly troublesome as more and more cases of pedophilia came to light in different countries. As the problems grew worse and his strength declined, he seemed to lack the energy to keep going.

In the United States the cases of pedophilia scandalized public opinion. By 2002, child sex-abuse claims had been filed, and the Catholic Church had to pay millions of dollars in indemnities; by 2008 the stories were constant television and newspaper material. Cases of pedophilia are not unique to Catholicism. They exist in Protestant churches and Jewish synagogues as well, but the statistics are much greater within the Catholic Church. Benedict XVI's visit to the United States in April 2008 seemed to stir up the controversy even more.

During that trip, Benedict XVI spoke directly to the problem and promised that the guilty priests would be excluded from the Church. Yet new accusations of pedophilia surfaced in Ireland in 2009, igniting the debates once again. The pope convened all the diocesan bishops of Ireland to the Vatican in 2010 to discuss the island's pedophile cases.

Another issue that grieved and wore the pope down was the famous case of Vatileaks, in which several secret papers of the Vatican were made public. The scandal began at the end of January 2012, when an Italian television program reported to have possession of Vatican papers involving Carlo Maria Viganò and an investigation for fraudulent dealings that had cost the Vatican millions of euros. To the shock of the Vatican, the Italian press began publishing the leaked documents.

In March 2012, the Vatican named an internal commission to investigate the papers. The commission discovered that Paolo Gabriele, the pope's personal butler since 2006 and a man in his confidence, had been leaking the documents. The commission's report was delivered to Pope Francis when he assumed the papacy. It appears that on December 17, 2012, Benedict

XVI also received the report from the internal investigation. After Gabriele's conviction, Benedict XVI pardoned him.

On February 11, 2013, in a routine canonization ceremony, Pope Benedict XVI announced in Latin something no one expected yet many sensed might be coming: he resigned his position. He also announced that his resignation would not go into effect until February 28, 2013, at 8:00 p.m.

Spanish journalist and author Eric Frattini has written several books about the Catholic Church and the papacy. A few hours after Benedict XVI's resignation announcement, Frattini commented:

He does not have health problems. John Paul II had health problems. He is a man with a few ailments but no real health problems. But Benedict XVI did not want to be pope. Before going into the conclave he had ordered his assistants to get the house ready to move back to Bavaria because he was going to leave the Vatican machinery behind. But the Holy Spirit called him to be pope.

He basically took out all the trash and, in so doing, prepared the way for the next man. He focused on cleaning up. He has been a revolutionary and cleansing pope. He faced the pedophile cases head-on instead of covering them up, and he has tried to clean up the Vatican Bank. . . . That is how he cleared the path for his successor.[3]

As Frattini indicates, Pope Benedict XVI's courage is laudable, yet the Catholic Church's image has deteriorated under his papacy.

The explanation Benedict XVI offered for his resignation had to do exclusively with his age and health:

After having repeatedly examined my conscience before God, I have come to the certainty that my strengths, due to an advanced age, are no longer suited to an adequate exercise of the Petrine ministry. . . . For this reason, and well aware of the seriousness of this act, with full freedom I declare that I renounce the ministry of Bishop of Rome, Successor of Saint Peter. . . .

Dear Brothers, I thank you most sincerely for all the love and work with which you have supported me in my ministry and I ask pardon for all my defects.[4]

Given the rarity of a pope's resignation,

everyone was taken by surprise. Thousands of questions sprang up in media around the globe. Was Benedict XVI trying to send the Catholic Church in a new direction and change the scenery of scandal? Did he feel that his efforts to continue John Paul II's work had come to an end? Did he think his limited strength made him incapable of carrying out the great movement of New Evangelization?

CAN A POPE RESIGN?

Although extremely rare, it is constitutionally acceptable for a pontiff to step down from his responsibilities voluntarily, as explained in chapter 7's discussion of papal elections and the causes of *sede vacante.* The previous pope, John Paul II, had not resigned despite being seriously ill. Benedict XVI had praised his predecessor's courage in dealing with suffering and upholding his responsibilities to the last breath:

> Yes, one can lead while suffering. Without a doubt, it is an extraordinary thing. But after a long pontificate and such an active life as pope, it was a meaningful and eloquent time of suffering that turned into something of a leadership style.[5]

As evident in his resignation announcement, Pope Benedict XVI proffered physical debility and age as the reasons for stepping down, though the real reasons may have been closer to what the magazine *Civiltà Cattolica*[6] asserts: "The pope is resigning his Petrine ministry not because he feels weak but because he perceives that the crucial difficulties at play require fresh energy."[7]

Even though a papal resignation, *renuntiatio pontificalis,* is not unheard of in pontificates or in history, the instances have been few and far between. First of all, a resignation must be voluntary. It is not recorded anywhere within canonical law to whom a pope must present his resignation, but since the eighteenth century, canonical law specialists have agreed that it is best to do so to the College of Cardinals.

The first papal resignation was in the third century under Pope Pontius. Next was Marcellinus in the beginning of the fourth century, followed by Liberius nearly fifty years later. After that, no pope resigned until the eleventh century, when Pope John XVIII resigned to retire to a monastery. In the eleventh century Pope Benedict IX also resigned but resumed the papacy a year later. In the thirteenth century, Pope Celestine V resigned, and finally Pope Gregory XII stepped down in 1415. Six hundred years passed without a papal resignation. Pope Pius VII did sign a letter of resignation under threats from Napoleon, and Pius XII did the same in case he should be captured by the Nazis. Neither of these letters had to be put into effect, however. Though it certainly raised many questions, Benedict XVI's resignation was totally legal and thus removed uncertainties the Catholic Church can face in the situation of *sede vacante*.

THE RESIGNATION AND CONVENING THE CONCLAVE

Pope Benedict XVI set the final day of his pontificate to be February 28, 2013. At his announcement the immense machinery of the Vatican got to work, organizing the second conclave of the twenty-first century.

Pope Benedict XVI continued his scheduled activities in the days following the announcement of his resignation, but nothing was the same. Thousands of pilgrims and journalists began to descend upon Rome to witness the change in pontificate. For Catholic believers this event, which occurs perhaps a few times during a person's life, is immensely important.

On February 27, Pope Benedict XVI held his final audience. The next day at 4:55 p.m., he left for the papal summer home in Castel Gandolfo, where he planned to stay for two months. From there he gave his final speech as pope. After his stay in Castel Gandolfo, the former Pope Benedict XVI planned to live in the Mater Ecclesiae monastery in Vatican City. His papal ring was scratched to invalidate it for signing Vatican documents. The problem of address arose after the announcement of Benedict XVI's resignation. Once a new pope was elected, what should Benedict XVI be called — Pope Emeritus or Roman Pontificate Emeritus?

THE BEGINNING OF THE CONCLAVE

The Vatican camerlengo, Tarcisio Bertone, presided over the conclave of 2013, scheduled to begin March 12. The cardinals did not want too much time to pass between the resignation of Benedict XVI and the election of the new pope. The needs of the Catholic Church demanded a prompt election. In the midst of the New Evangelization project, the church needed a visible head and a dynamic leader to guide it.

The first step to convening the conclave of the College of Cardinals involved calling all cardinals under eighty years of age. Generally a conclave occurs between fifteen to twenty days after the Holy See is vacated. In the case of Benedict XVI's *sede vacante,* the process could be expedited since there were no funeral rites or ceremonies to be held. Furthermore, because it was a resignation, the cardinals were aware beforehand of the date the see would be vacated.

To accelerate the date of the conclave, and since the majority of the cardinals were already in Rome to bid farewell to Benedict XVI, the pope himself issued a *motu proprio* on February 25, authorizing the College of Cardinals to set a date for the conclave. The date initially chosen was March 4. After a week of deliberations and while waiting on the 115 cardinals eligible to vote and to be elected, the date for the beginning of the conclave was pushed back to March 14. In the continual juggling of the dates, the conclave ended up being slated to begin on March 12. From that moment on the cardinals would be isolated until the new pope was elected.

The 115 cardinals came from five continents. Sixty were from Europe, thirty-three from the American continent, eleven from Africa, and the other eleven from Asia and Oceania, with two cardinals absent.

In the conclave of 2013, there were twenty-five possible popes being discussed, several from North America, a few from Latin America and Italy, and one African. The talk centered around six men, though the number varies according to different sources.

Archbishop Gerhard Mueller, responsible for the Congregation for the Doctrine of the Faith, told several media outlets, "I know a lot of bishops and cardinals from Latin America who could take responsibility for the universal Church."[8]

Some were already predicting that the pope would not be from Europe. Mueller had previously told the *Rheinische Post,* "The universal Church teaches that Christianity isn't centered on Europe."[9]

On this matter the Swiss cardinal Kurt Koch commented, "I can imagine taking a step towards a black pope, an African pope or a Latin American pope. I can imagine this."[10]

The Mexican website *El Economista* published on December 17, 2012, this summarized list of papal candidates:

- João Braz de Aviz (Brazil, age 65). He supports the preferential option for the poor of Latin American liberation theology but not to the extreme of some of liberation theology's proponents. His low profile could work against him.

- Timothy Dolan (USA, age 62). He became the voice of US Catholicism after being named archbishop of New York in 2009.
- Marc Ouellet (Canada, age 68). He is currently the functioning chief director of staff of the Vatican as prefect of the Congregation for Bishops.
- Gianfranco Ravasi (Italy, age 70). He has been the president of the Pontifical Council for Culture since 2007 and represents the Catholic Church in the worlds of science, art, and culture, even among atheists.
- Leonardo Sandri (Argentina, age 69). He is a "transatlantic" figure, born in Buenos Aires of Italian parents.
- Odilo Pedro Scherer (Brazil, age 63). He is the strongest Latin American candidate. The archbishop of São Paulo, the largest diocese in the largest Catholic nation, he is conservative within Brazil but would be considered moderate elsewhere.
- Christoph Schoenborn (Austria, age 67). He is a former student of Pope

Benedict XVI but has a pastoral nature that the previous pope lacked.

- Angelo Scola (Italy, age 71). He is archbishop of Milan, considered a stepping-stone for the papacy, and the main candidate for many Italians.
- Luis Tagle (Philippines, age 55). His charisma earns him comparisons with the late John Paul II.
- Peter Turkson (Ghana, age 64). He is the main African candidate. He is the president of the Pontifical Council for Justice and Peace, the spokesperson for the Catholic Church's social conscience, and supports worldwide financial reform.[11]

The list, indicative of candidate speculation in many other newspapers and journals, including the March 10, 2013, list published in the *New York Times,* did not even mention Jorge Mario Bergoglio. The Argentine press outlet *El Clarín* barely referenced Bergoglio as a possible candidate. Only one article came out about the Argentine cardinal; in a brief profile, on March 12, 2013, he was mentioned as gaining ground in a possible election.

Why did no one focus on Bergoglio, who had received the second-highest number of votes in the conclave of 2005? Perhaps, once again, Bergoglio's discreet presence let him slide unnoticed by the press, both around the world and in his own country.

THE VOTING

The first day of voting, March 12, 2013, ended in *fumata nera,* as was to be expected. It seems that many of the papal candidates, including Angelo Scola and Odilo Scherer, garnered very few ballots. The Italian Scola represented the conservative wing more closely aligned with the mechanisms of the Vatican State while Scherer, the Brazilian cardinal, represented the reformers.

From the very first round of voting, however, the candidate with the greatest support above all, from American and European votes, was Bergoglio.[12] Cardinal Timothy Dolan, archbishop of New York, seemingly asked his colleagues from North America to vote for Bergoglio. At dinner the first evening there was a great deal of talk about whether Scola would be the best pope. André Vingt-trois, the archbishop of Paris, who heavily influenced European votes, reportedly said that Bergoglio was a better solution than Scola.[13]

In the preparatory sessions a few days earlier, Bergoglio had spoken of the mercy of the Catholic Church and the need for spiritual renewal. Though the archbishop of Buenos Aires is not known as an orator, his words penetrated to the heart. He concluded by citing the need to "be done with the career-driven mentality of promotions and positions of power."[14]

In the first round of voting that morning, it seemed that some Asian and African votes were directed to Bergoglio. The following day, Wednesday, March 13, 2013, he garnered even more ballots. It also seemed that the American votes were directed toward Bergoglio, as well as most European votes, but Italy has the greatest number of cardinals of any country in the world, leaving much to be decided.

In the fourth and final voting round of the conclave, in the afternoon session, the Argentine received a landslide ninety votes, six more than Benedict XVI had received in 2005. At 7:05 p.m. the much anticipated *fumata bianca* appeared. The new pope was the Argentine cardinal Jorge Mario Bergoglio, who, a few moments later, adopted the name Francis in honor of St. Francis of Assisi, close friend of the poor and founder of the Franciscan order. In choosing this name Bergoglio made it clear from the beginning where his loyalties lay. He would break with the ostentation and show of Rome that had done so much damage to the image of the church of the poor, the church of the people.

Pope Francis, of Jesuit background and with a clear vocation for the Christian and especially Catholic people, was the first Latin American pontiff.

The new pope was proclaimed by cardinal protodeacon Jean-Louis Pierre Tauran with the Latin formula:

Annuntio vobis gaudium magnum;
habemus Papam:
Eminentissimum ac Reverendissimum
    Dominum,
Dominum Georgium Marium
Sanctae Romanae Ecclesiae Cardinalem
    Bergoglio
qui sibi nomen imposuit Franciscum.[15]

The first words of Pope Francis shot like lightning from St. Peter's Square to the far reaches of the world:

Brothers and sisters, good evening!
    You know that it was the duty of the Conclave to give Rome a Bishop. It seems that my brother Cardinals have gone to the ends of the earth to get

one . . . but here we are . . . I thank you for your welcome. The diocesan community of Rome now has its Bishop. Thank you!

And first of all, I would like to offer a prayer for our Bishop Emeritus, Benedict XVI. Let us pray together for him, that the Lord may bless him and that Our Lady may keep him.

Our Father . . .

Hail Mary . . .

Glory Be . . .

And now, we take up this journey: Bishop and People. This journey of the Church of Rome which presides in charity over all the Churches. A journey of fraternity, of love, of trust among us. Let us always pray for one another. Let us pray for the whole world, that there may be a great spirit of fraternity. It is my hope for you that this journey of the Church, which we start today, and in which my Cardinal Vicar, here present, will assist me, will be fruitful for the evangelization of this most beautiful city.

And now I would like to give the blessing, but first — first I ask a favour of you: before the Bishop blesses his people, I ask you to pray to the Lord that he will bless me: the prayer of the people asking the blessing for their Bishop. Let us make, in silence, this prayer: your prayer over me.

[. . .]

Now I will give the Blessing to you and to the whole world, to all men and women of goodwill.

[Blessing]

Brothers and sisters, I leave you now. Thank you for your welcome. Pray for me and until we meet again. We will see each other soon. Tomorrow I wish to go and pray to Our Lady, that she may watch over all of Rome. Good night and sleep well![16]

The three most interesting features of this speech are:

1. "To the ends of the earth." With this phrase Pope Francis wanted a way to demonstrate the universality of the Catholic Church and the end of Rome and Europe as the epicenter of the Catholic Church for nearly two thousand years.

2. "Bishop and People." The Christian people must return to their lost role as protagonists since they are a fundamental part of the Catholic

Church. In one sense, Pope Francis elevated the people to the same status as the Roman Curia.

3. Prayer of the people. Pope Francis sought the prayers of the Christian people, thus revealing one of his charismas: prayer as a source of renewal for the Catholic Church.

The Argentine son of Italian immigrants, the chemistry student, the Jesuit priest, the professor, the auxiliary bishop of Buenos Aires, the outspoken archbishop now holds the future of the Catholic Church in his hands. What will his first steps be? How will he leave his mark on the Catholic Church? What will he do in his mission to fight poverty and the ostentation of the Vatican? What will his main directives be?

■ ■ ■ ■

PART III
FIVE CHALLENGES

■ ■ ■ ■

Chapter 9
The First Pope
from the Americas

For on a certain day, when he had gone forth to meditate in the fields, he was walking nigh the church of Saint Damian, which from all its exceeding great age was threatening to fall, and, at the prompting of the Spirit, went within to pray. Prostrating himself before an Image of the Crucified, he was filled with no small consolation of spirit as he prayed. And as with eyes full of tears he gazed upon the Lord's Cross, he heard with his bodily ears a Voice proceeding from that Cross, saying thrice: "Francis, go and repair My house, which, as thou seest, is falling utterly into ruin." Francis trembled, being alone in the church, and was astonied [*sic*] at the sound of such a wondrous Voice, and, perceiving in his heart the might of divine speech, was carried out of himself into ecstasy. When at length he came unto himself again, he prepared to obey, and devoted himself wholly unto the behest to repair the material church; howbeit, the principal intent of the message had regard unto that Church which Christ had purchased with His own blood, even as the Holy Spirit taught him, and as he himself afterward revealed unto the Brethren.[1]

A few minutes after being elected pope on March 13, 2013, when Jorge Mario Bergoglio announced his new name, many around him were probably taken aback. The most common practice is for a pope to inherit the name of a pontiff who has preceded him, thus identifying with his charisma and mission. The case of John Paul II is one of the most significant. He took his name after the premature death of John Paul I as a sign of the continuation of his apostolic work. Benedict XVI was inspired by Benedict XV, the pope between world wars. So why would a pope of Jesuit background choose the name of the founder of the Franciscan order? Beyond that, why would he not choose the complete title "Francis I"? Could it be that he thought the name by itself would sound more down-to-earth?

Pope Francis is the first pope in history not to use a number to identify himself among possible successors. Vatican spokesman Federico Lombardi has confirmed that his name would automatically become Francis I should a future pope also choose the name Francis. Yet the question remained, why would a Jesuit take a Franciscan name? St. Ignatius of Loyola was also a man dedicated to the poor and who highly valued the vow of poverty. Pope Francis provided the answer:

During the election, I was seated next to the Archbishop Emeritus of São Paolo and Prefect Emeritus of the Congregation for the Clergy, Cardinal Claudio Hummes: a good friend, a good friend! When things were looking dangerous, he encouraged me. And when the votes reached two thirds, there was the usual applause, because the Pope had been elected. And he gave me a hug and a kiss, and said: "Don't forget the poor!" And those words came to me: the poor, the poor. Then, right away, thinking of the poor, I thought of Francis of Assisi. Then I thought of all the wars, as the votes were still being counted, till the end. Francis is also the man of peace. That is how the name came into my heart: Francis of Assisi. For me, he is the man of poverty, the man of peace, the man who loves and protects creation.[2]

Pope Francis's reasons are abundantly clear. Reading the account of St. Francis of Assisi's calling before the crucifix at St. Damian in St. Bonaventure's *Life of Saint Francis* provides more context. The new pope's mission is deeper and more difficult than just drawing the church closer to the poor: " 'Francis, go and repair My house, which, as thou seest, is falling utterly into ruin.' "[3] The order given to St. Francis is both the signal of an alarm and a plea: "Go and repair My house."

Will Pope Francis be a reforming pope?

FRANCIS, POPE OF REFORMS

The current pope's predecessors were not innovators. It is true that John Paul II had a special charisma, but he did not bring about any significant change or reform in the practices or heart of the Catholic Church.

The structure of the Catholic Church has remained fixed for centuries, and the Second Vatican Council's attempts at transformation were only partially realized. Changes were definitely made within liturgy, the laity was elevated to a greater role in some realms, and the political and economic systems of the Catholic Church were modernized in some instances, but the majority of the proposed reforms were all for naught.

Pope John Paul I's program of reform was much more ambitious in the few weeks of his pontificate than that of the much longer papacies of John Paul II and Benedict XVI. John Paul I did away with the pontifical style of indirect speech and the use of the royal "we" in his discourses, opting for a more direct, common language. He dispensed of the practice of receiving official visitors from the *sedia gestatoria,* a portable throne. He thus retired the image of the pope as the monarch of the Church, which had been in place since the Middle Ages.

The motto for John Paul I's pontificate was *Humilitas,* "humility," as reflected in his refusal to wear the papal tiara[4] in a coronation ceremony, preferring instead a simple papal inaugural mass. John Paul II and Benedict XVI followed his lead and also avoided these practices. One of John Paul I's most controversial statements was, "He [God] is our father; even more he is our mother,"[5] in reference to the Scripture texts in Isaiah 49:14–15.[6] His greatest contribution, however, was an encyclical that attempted to give unprecedented momentum to the Second Vatican Council, hoping that its relaunch would become an event of historic proportions.

He also sought reforms within the Curia and the priesthood and pushed for the redistribution of the Catholic Church's material wealth, requiring the richest churches to give 1 percent to churches in the developing world. In the political sphere, John Paul I was a fighter. When Jorge Rafael Videla, the Argentine dictator, visited the Vatican, the pope remonstrated with him concerning the human rights violations in his country.

Pope Francis seems to fit more with this casual style of papacy than with Benedict XVI's more formal, sober air. Some of the new pope's actions are already delineating his focus. In his first homily to the cardinals and believers, he concentrated on St. Joseph, the husband of the Virgin Mary, the custodian or protector of Jesus and Mary when they were in danger. Regarding St. Joseph's protection, Pope Francis extrapolated for the world today:

The vocation of being a "protector," however, is not just something involving us Christians alone; it also has a prior dimension which is simply human, involving everyone. It means protecting all creation, the beauty of the created world, as the Book of Genesis tells us and as Saint Francis of Assisi showed us. It means respecting each of God's creatures and respecting the environment in which we live.[7]

Pope Francis developed this vocation of protecting in four areas: concern for each and every person in love, concern for the family, development of sincere friendships, and care of God's creation. In this homily, spoken in front of many political representatives from around the world, he specially emphasized the responsibility of governments in the work of protection:

Please, I would like to ask all those who have positions of responsibility in economic, political and social life, and all men and women of goodwill: let us be "protectors" of creation, protectors of God's plan inscribed in nature, protectors of one another and of the environment. Let us not allow omens of destruction and death to accompany the advance of this world![8]

He also remarked on the importance of cultivating the interior self. If we do not take care of ourselves, we will be hard pressed to protect those around us:

But to be "protectors," we also have to keep watch over ourselves! Let us not forget that hatred, envy and pride defile our lives! Being protectors, then, also means keeping watch over our emotions, over our hearts, because they are the seat of good and evil intentions: intentions that build up and tear down! We must not be afraid of goodness or even tenderness![9]

Finally the pope appealed to the courage of loving and being tender to those around us so that no one will think love is weaker than hate or bitterness.

Here I would add one more thing: caring, protecting, demands goodness, it calls for a certain tenderness. In the Gospels, Saint Joseph appears as a strong and courageous man, a working man, yet in his heart we see great tenderness, which is not the virtue of the weak but rather a sign of strength of spirit and a capacity for concern, for compassion, for genuine openness to others, for love. We must not be afraid of goodness, of tenderness![10]

Pope Francis concluded with a message of hope, referring to Romans 4:18, which describes how the patriarch Abraham believed: "who, contrary to hope, in hope believed, so that he became the father of many nations, according to what was spoken, 'So shall your descendants be.' " This homily confronts a society heaped in material possessions with a spirit of protection and care, which God has bestowed for all humanity.

Another of the pope's first gestures was to reject the golden fisherman's ring with which the pope traditionally seals official Vatican documents. He has opted for a more modest silver ring. He also exchanged the gold cross the pope typically wears for an iron cross. And he has thus far refused the "popemobile," a specially designed motor vehicle used for outdoor public appearances. A variety of these vehicles allows the Vatican to select an appropriate mode of transportation for the pope, depending upon level of security, distance, and speed. For his first day in office, Pope Francis traveled by police car. In his first pass through St. Peter's Square, he got out on several occasions to greet the people, more interested in being close to the believers than in his personal safety.

These actions indicate the pope's disposition, but will they remain mere gestures? The question can be answered only as Pope Francis spends more time in office. What is certain is that as archbishop of Buenos Aires, he waved off the archbishop's palace, a comfortable residence near the home of the nation's president, and commonly traveled by public transportation.

Pope Francis is doubtless a simple man, willing to speak to anyone. Aldo Cagnoli, a pilot for the Italian airline Alitalia, got to know Bergoglio on his frequent visits to Rome. He describes the current pope as an exemplary man who, instead of building walls and hiding behind his knowledge or his position, knows how to face criticism; as a man who respects his neighbors and is always open to learning.[11]

Counter to modern-day values, which measure a man's greatness based on his position, bank account, or fame, Cagnoli promptly discovered the greatness inherent in Bergoglio's service and humility, as he expressed frankly to journalists Sergio Rubin and Francesca Ambrogetti:

His greatness lies in his simplicity together with his great wisdom, his sympathy together with his seriousness, his mental openness together with his uprightness, his ability to listen and learn from everyone while still having something to teach. I think he accomplishes quite simply, although at the same time extraordinarily, what many men both within and outside of the church ought to do but, sadly, do not.[12]

If Pope Francis has so many virtues, why, as previously asked, was he not among the favorites nearing the conclave? Perhaps society at large and the Catholic hierarchy itself thought that the Catholic Church needed a hinge pope, one who could overcome the current church crises but not a reformer who would change the core shape and institutions of the Catholic Church.

AN AGENDA SET BY OTHERS

The entire world is watching Pope Francis, hoping that he initiates immediate, visible change in different spheres of the Catholic Church. The pope himself naturally has longer-term projects that do not go in the populist direction that mass media is hoping for. We must not forget that Pope Francis is quite conservative in terms of doctrine and will not make an abrupt change of course in some of the most pressing matters.

The majority of newspapers and news media focus on four main issues: the pedophile scandals, transparency in Vatican affairs, the Catholic Church's stance on social matters (homosexual marriage, abortion, euthanasia, etc.), and the decline in Church membership worldwide.[13] To these issues, some also add interfaith dialogue.

The Pedophile Scandals

The scandals naturally concern the Catholic Church, but Benedict XVI already took the principle necessary measures, and all that is left to Francis is the execution of the same policies and certain gestures toward those ultimately responsible.

Sexual scandals are nothing new. In the 1950s, there had been several cases reported, leading Father Gerald Fitzgerald to found a religious order that helped abused children and treated the perpetrating priests. Fitzgerald had originally begun his ministry to help priests who fell victim to alcohol or drugs but soon discovered the need to treat priests who had abused minors.

Father Gerald was one of the first to warn the church hierarchy of the need to act immediately to face the problem. In a 1952 letter to Bishop Robert Dwyer of Reno, Nevada, Fitzgerald said:

> I myself would be inclined to favor laicization for any priest, upon objective evidence, for tampering with the virtue of the young, my argument being, from this point onward the charity to the Mystical Body should take precedence over charity to the individual. . . . Moreover, in practice, real conversions will be found to be extremely rare. . . . Hence, leaving them on duty or wandering from diocese to diocese is contributing to scandal or at least to the approximate danger of scandal.[14]

The Saint Luke Institute was created to treat priests with these and similar types of problems. The statistics of this service center are impressive. From 1985 to 2008, 365 priests underwent treatment for pedophilia, and only 6 percent, or 22 priests in all, had a relapse. Father Fitzgerald even worked on plans for a residence for pedophile priests on an island in Barbados, focused on their seclusion and rehabilitation. It would also have been a type of penitentiary for the most severe cases. But after Fitzgerald's death, the project never came to completion.

In the last few years in the United States alone, there have been some three thousand civil charges for cases of pedophilia brought against the Catholic Church.[15] In March 2010, this figure was also recognized by the Vatican prosecutor, Monsignor Charles J. Scicluna.[16] In that same interview, Scicluna also confirmed that the Catholic Church has tallied the cases back to 1922, the year the famous document *Crimen sollicitationis* (the crime of soliciting) was published.[17]

After the first interventions of Pope Pius XI, Pope John XXIII revised the instructions to intervene in cases of pedophilia. Official declarations regarding this topic date back to 1962, when Cardinal Alfredo Ottaviani, secretary of the Congregation for the Doctrine of the Faith, sent an order to archbishops, bishops, and patriarchs to watch out for this issue and send any relevant case to the offices of the congregation.

Pope John Paul II, in declarations made April 23, 2002, condemned the pedophile priests:

I too have been deeply grieved by the fact that priests and religious, whose vocation it is to help people live holy lives in the sight of God, have themselves caused such suffering and scandal to the young. Because of the great harm done by some priests and religious, the Church herself is viewed with distrust, and many are offended at the way in which the Church's leaders are perceived to have acted in this matter.[18]

In the same message he acknowledged the Church's errors in dealing with the issue:

It is true that a generalized lack of knowledge of the nature of the problem and also at times the advice of clinical experts led Bishops to make decisions which subsequent events showed to be wrong.[19]

Pope Benedict XVI also addressed the subject on various occasions and is the pope who took the most steps toward halting the terrible practice. In November 2005, he published a polemical document called "Instruction Concerning the Criteria for the Discernment of Vocations with regard to Persons with Homosexual Tendencies."

From the beginning of Benedict XVI's pontificate, the efforts to contain the problem accelerated, yet scandals continued coming to light in numerous countries, including Canada, Ireland, the United Kingdom, Mexico, Belgium, France, Germany, and Australia. These cases caused the resignation of several ecclesial leaders, including Cardinal Hans Hermann Groër, archbishop of Vienna, accused of sexually abusing minors. One of the most scandalous cases was the conviction of Father Marcial Maciel of Mexico, founder of the Legion of Christ.

Between 1950 and 2002, the problem seems to have affected an estimated 10,667 victims with 4,392 priests accused, of which 3,000 are currently under investigation. The Catholic Church has recognized some 4,000 cases in the last ten years.[20] In the past few years cases have come to light in the developing world as well, particularly in Africa and Asia.

What is Pope Francis's position on the matter? He sees no relationship between this issue and priestly celibacy. He believes that in the majority of instances, pedophilia occurs in the most intimate setting, the home. Many fathers, stepfathers, and uncles are abusers; therefore, Pope Francis holds that the perpetrator is pathologically sick and that he was so before becoming a priest.[21] He also believes immediate action must be taken in cases of pedophilia:

> If the priest is a pedophile, he was
> already a pedophile before becoming a
> priest. Now, when this happens, we can
> never turn a blind eye. You cannot be in
> a position of power and destroy someone
> else's life. In my diocese I have never
> faced this problem, but once a bishop
> called to ask what he should do in a situ-
> ation like that, and I told him he had to
> take away their licenses, that they could
> no longer exercise the priesthood, and
> to start a canonical investigation. . . .
> For me, that's the approach to take. I
> don't buy in to perspectives that preach
> a certain corporate spirit to protect an
> untarnished image of the institution. . . .
> Recently we've learned about cases in
> Ireland that have been going on for
> about twenty years, and the current pope
> clearly said, "Zero tolerance with this
> crime." I recognize Benedict XVI's cour-
> age and integrity in this matter.[22]

Bergoglio reportedly put these principles
into practice as soon as he assumed papal
responsibilities. The Italian daily *Il Fatto
Quotidiano* reported that Pope Francis
rebuffed Cardinal Bernard Law, the former

archbishop of Boston who resigned in 2002 over the scandals in his diocese. He had protected some 250 pedophile priests between 1984 and 2002. When Cardinal Law wanted to approach the pope to congratulate him, Pope Francis's face fell, and he reportedly said, "He is not to come to this church any more."[23]

Though not confirmed by the Vatican, *Il Fatto Quotidiano* reported that Pope Francis is preparing to send Law to a cloistered monastery.[24]

Transparency in Vatican Affairs

Scandals unleashed by the so-called Vatileaks still have the Roman Curia shaken up. No one as yet knows what the new pope's first reaction was on receiving the internal report.[25] A Vatican spokesperson said that Pope Francis had not yet had time to read the reports,[26] but given the new pope's character, he will not delay in taking appropriate measures.

The Vatileaks report was compiled by a commission created in the spring of 2012 by Pope Benedict XVI. Three cardinals — Jozef Tomko, Salvatore De Giorgi, and the Spanish Julián Herranz — comprised the commission. They reportedly questioned thirty people and delivered their report in

December 2012 to the former pope. Some cardinals requested to see the report before the conclave of 2013 but were denied.

What is in this famous report? Some writers, like Eric Frattini, talk about an internal struggle within Vatican City between supporters of Tarsacio Bertone, Benedict XVI's secretary who enjoyed a special understanding with the former pope, and Cardinal Angelo Sodano, dean of the College of Cardinals.[27] Italian author Gianluigi Nuzzi's 2012 sensation *Sua Santità. Le carte segrete di Benedetto XVI* (*His Holiness: The Secret Papers of Benedict XVI*) provides details about the pope's private affairs, his letters, and confidential memos. Some of the papers mention embezzlement and fraud within the Holy See. The book also references the scandal of a supposed donation from the former president of the RAI (Radiotelevisione italiana, Italy's public broadcasting network) upon Pope Benedict XVI's concession of an audience as well as compromising information about the Legion of Christ and its founder. All of these documents were apparently stolen and leaked by Paolo Gabriele, Pope Benedict XVI's personal butler.

When asked in an interview if the Vatileaks might have played a part in the choice of a non-Italian pope, the cardinal of Lima, Cipriani Thorne, commented,

I believe so. The truth is we don't know much about it. But yes, there has been a climate of saying, well, we have to get straight what's happened here and clean it up. Evidently, for A or for B, those who are closest in some way have been somewhat pushed to the side, but not like in an agreement, nor being blamed for anything. But yes, this element has been present.[28]

The archbishop of Lima further commented on his reaction to the election of Pope Francis,

But yes, he [Francis] will give us a sign once he starts choosing his people, his aides. I think there's an outcry from the cardinals to simplify many things in the Curia, to increase transparency, and to be closer to the believing public.[29]

For now, Pope Francis has provisionally confirmed Tarsicio Bertone in the position of papal secretary, but many believe the new pope will eventually form his own team.

In terms of Vatican finances and a hypothetical sale of church antiques or a poorer institutional church, Pope Francis thinks that at times people confuse a museum, which is what the Vatican is, with a place coated in gold. Yet since religion needs money to keep going, the pope says,

> The thing is the way you use money given as tithe or donations. The Vatican's balance is public, and it always shows a deficit: what comes in from donations or from visits to the museum goes to the leprosarium, to schools, to African, Asian, and American communities.[30]

Regarding the *Banco Ambrosiano,* Pope Francis praised Pope John Paul II's actions of openly condemning the Italian bank's schemes.[31] Though, as previously discussed, it seems certain that the new pope intends to do away with ostentation, true charity for him is not self-serving. In many charity events people selfishly seek to serve their own ends above doing good to others. Pope Francis sees this approach as the antithesis of charity. He maintains that true love means putting ourselves in the service of our neighbor whom we claim to love. Otherwise, it is a mere caricature of true charity.[32] For him, the poor are the real treasure of the Catholic Church.[33]

The Catholic Church's Stance on Social Matters (Homosexual Marriage and Abortion)

Though he by no means thinks exactly like his predecessors, the new pope does fall along the conservative line of the previous two popes. The issues of homosexual marriage and defense of the family have been two of the Catholic Church's battle horses in the last decade. The official position on homosexuality is set: the Church condemns homosexual practice but not the person.

In 1975, the Congregation for the Doctrine of the Faith declared,

> For according to the objective moral order, homosexual relations are acts which lack an essential and indispensable finality. In Sacred Scripture they are condemned as a serious depravity and even presented as the sad consequence of rejecting God.[34]

The Catholic Church makes a distinction between homosexual orientation, or homosexuality, and homosexual activity, or homosexualism. The Church teaches that homosexual orientation is not a sin in and of itself but that it can lead to actions that are considered sin. In 1995, the Congregation for the Doctrine of the Faith published a response to certain laws in the United States especially in regard to homosexual marriage and the adoption of children:

> Homosexual persons, as human persons, have the same rights as all persons including the right of not being treated in a manner which offends their personal dignity. . . . Among other rights, all persons have the right to work, to housing, etc. Nevertheless, these rights are not absolute. They can be legitimately limited for objectively disordered external conduct. . . . There are areas in which it is not unjust discrimination to take sexual orientation into account, for example, in the placement of children for adoption or foster care, in employment of teachers or athletic coaches, and in military recruitment. . . . "Sexual orientation" does not constitute a quality comparable to race, ethnic background, etc. in respect to non-discrimination. Unlike these, homosexual orientation is an objective disorder.[35]

Pope Francis's opinions regarding homosexual marriage are closely aligned with the

Catholic Church's official rulings. For him, the Bible eloquently expresses the basis of natural law and recognizes only the union between a man and a woman. He acknowledges that homosexuality has always existed. It has been a historic reality since antiquity, yet the difference today is our attitude toward homosexuality. Pope Francis thinks that today's world has turned a civil union between two men into a "marriage" with comparable rights and relational status. He holds that this state of affairs is merely an anthropological setback that diminishes the value of traditional marriage.[36]

The pope's opinion is also set regarding the adoption of children by homosexual couples:

> If there is a private union, there is no third party nor is society affected. Now, if the union is given the category of marriage and thus permitted to adopt, children are going to be affected. Everyone needs a male father and a female mother to help them develop their identity.[37]

Abortion is another polemical issue in today's society. In defense of life and the rights of the fetus, the Catholic Church fights to stop laws that permit abortive practices. The Congregation for the Doctrine of the Faith addressed the topic in its declaration on abortion. The document initially spoke about the defense of life, citing a verse from the book of Wisdom: "Death was not God's doing, he takes no pleasure in the extinction of the living" (1:13).[38] The report then gave several reasons for the defense of life:

In the Didache it is clearly said: "You shall not kill by abortion the fruit of the womb and you shall not murder the infant already born." . . . Athenagoras emphasizes that Christians consider as murderers those women who take medicines to procure an abortion; he condemns the killers of children, including those still living in their mother's womb, "where they are already the object of the care of divine Providence." Tertullian did not always perhaps use the same language; he nevertheless clearly affirms the essential principle: "To prevent birth is anticipated murder; it makes little difference whether one destroys a life already born or does away with it in its nascent stage. The one who will be a man is already one."[39]

Since this document was written in 1974 and ratified by Pope Paul VI, Pope Francis could request that it be updated. His opinions on the matter closely reflect those put forth in the declaration, but his way of expressing it is somewhat different. For Pope Francis abortion is not a religious problem but a moral problem. He believes that when a new being is created, the new creature has his or her own DNA, a type of genetic responsibility that implies personhood. The problem then becomes scientific rather than theological, separated from religious morality in and of itself since impeding life is an ethical problem. The pope believes that the right to life is foremost, the most important of all rights, and that abortion is killing someone who cannot defend him- or herself.[40]

Declining Church Membership Worldwide

One of the Catholic Church's most pressing problems is the decline in the number of its adherents and in those seeking the priesthood. Though the Church continues growing in continents like Africa and Asia, the decline is quite noticeable in Europe, North America, and Latin America. Why has there been such a steep drop in membership? There are numerous explanations. In Europe, particularly in the countries with a long Catholic tradition like Italy, Spain, and Portugal, the decline goes hand-in-hand with the staunch secularism of their societies.

In his visit to Spain, Benedict XVI referenced this "attack" on the faith from secularized society. In declarations made to Spanish bishops in July 2006, Benedict XVI said, "I am aware of, and I encourage the impulse that you are giving to pastoral activity at a time of rapid secularization, which can also affect the internal life of Christian communities."[41] Some countries like Poland seem to fight this decline in membership and priestly vocations. In Spain, however, 70.8 percent of the country claims to be Catholic, yet regarding practicing Catholics, the percentages drop: only 13.6 percent of Catholics go to mass once a week and 59.8 percent go rarely or never at all.[42] Other traditionally Catholic European countries report similar statistics.

The issue of priestly vocations is even more concerning throughout Europe. Theologian José María Vigil calls it a "collapse" of vocations. He references a statement by José María Mardones in the *Sal Terra* magazine that Europe seems to be headed to a point of "no return."[43]

The lack of new priests is no more dangerous than the aging of priests currently serving. The median age of priests in Europe is
sixty-five. While it is true that the median
age in Europe is high (41.1 years in Spain
alone)44 and that the population in general
is aging, the average age for priests is far
higher than that of the general populace.
Mardones suggests that an entire genera-
tion of priests might be lost, and this loss is
irreparable.[45]

The economic crisis in Europe has somewhat alleviated the dearth of aspiring priests
entering seminary. In Spain in 2011, the
number grew 4 percent over 2010's numbers, but the death rate of priests surpasses
the number of new priests ordained, resulting in the alarming statistic of an annual
loss of 200 priests. Foreigners and a few
cases of middle-aged men attending European seminaries reduce these margins a bit.
In 2010, only 122 priests were ordained in
all of Spain, and there were a total of 1,278
seminarians in Catholic seminaries.[46]

In more general statistics the number of
European priests is still greatest in terms of
the number of diocesans and those belonging to an order. Worldwide there are an
estimated 275,543 priests and 135,051
members of orders; in Europe those num-

bers are 133,997 and 57,058, respectively, higher than in any other region. The average number of parishioners per priest worldwide is 2,857.51. Throughout the globe there are 117,978 seminarians in seminaries for older men and 25,566 in seminaries for younger men. The difference is striking. Seminaries in Africa and Asia report higher numbers than those in Europe, closer to the numbers seen in the American continent.[47]

The case of women belonging to religious orders in the United States is also significant, dropping 50 percent within a little more than twenty-five years, from 181,000 in 1966 to 92,000 in 1993.[48]

The numbers of priests who marry or who abandon the priesthood for other causes must also be added to these statistics. In France the rate of ordination has decreased 8 percent annually since 1947.[49] And over a thirty-year period in the late twentieth century, some eighty thousand priests and religious men and women left their vocations worldwide.[50]

The decline in seminarians and followers in the Americas, particularly in Spanish- and Portuguese-speaking regions, is another chief concern of the Vatican. Some chalk up the decline to the requirements and limitations of celibacy. In Orthodoxy priests can be married if they were married before being ordained. Others point out that the Catholic Church limits its pool of resources by refusing to ordain women for priestly ministry, as is done in the Lutheran, Calvinist, Anglican, and majority of evangelical denominations.

Pope Francis is not closed off to the idea that at some point the celibacy requirement for priests might change. He believes that the discipline of celibacy will continue but should be formulated for cultural reasons, not as a universal option. His words seem to leave the subject only somewhat open-ended. Thus he says that celibacy is a matter not of faith but rather of discipline. It has been enforced by the Catholic Church since the year 1100. The pope's exact words on the topic are, "It might change."[51] This is, at least, much further than other members of the Catholic hierarchy, who will hear and speak nothing on the matter, have gone.

The hemorrhaging of the faithful from the Catholic Church in the Americas has intensified since the start in the 1970s. The Church has lost the largest number of followers in Brazil. In the 1990s, 75 percent of Brazilians claimed to be Catholic. By 2011, this number had dropped to 65 percent.[52]

Where did the Catholic parishioners go? The majority went to Protestant churches. Some statistics report up to 15.4 percent growth among Protestant churches.[53]

Anthropologist David Stoll had addressed the phenomenon in 1990, but others had seen it coming much earlier. Jesuit priest and author Prudencio Damboriena broached the topic in his 1962 book *El protestantismo en América Latina.*

Despite conversions from some sectors of Protestantism to Catholicism (among some Anglicans and Lutherans, for example), the Church of Rome continues to decline rapidly in Latin America. The decline in the United States is less precipitous, given the influx of Catholic immigrants and the return of some former Catholics after having spent part of their lives in Protestant churches. What is the secret to the spread of Protestantism? Why has the Catholic Church been unable to stop it? Previous chapters have mentioned how the Catholic Church has attempted to stanch this bloodletting but to no avail. Neither political influence nor attempts to evangelize have been sufficient up to now.

Pope Francis believes the secret lies in pastoral care, in being near the people and being more approachable, in better receiving the people who come to the Catholic Church. The Catholic Church in Argentina calls it a "cordial welcome." Pope Francis believes it is key for priests and all Catholics to go out to meet the people, just as in the biblical text the shepherd leaves the ninety-nine sheep in the pen and goes after the one lost lamb. Pope Francis believes that parishioners are not alienated so much by doctrine as by not feeling cared for. The Catholic Church, in his opinion, has to go out to the streets to look for people and get to know them by name to be able to preach the gospel to them.[54]

The movements of New Evangelization and the Evangelization of Culture are precisely along these lines. By being present out on the streets and having a larger cultural influence, the Church seeks to re-Christianize countries that, until relatively recently, considered themselves Christian. Pope Benedict XVI used the term *New Evangelization* when establishing the Pontifical Council for Promoting the New Evangelization on September 21, 2010.[55] He understood very clearly, shortly after being elected pope, that the desertions of Catholics in Europe and the Americas had to stop. It seemed he wanted to declare war on the reigning secularism, and his main weapon would be the New Evangelization.

Benedict XVI developed his plan and named Archbishop Salvatore Fisichella to head it up. The archbishop in turn sought the support of the most conservative sector of the Catholic Church, which is also the sector currently growing the fastest, the Neocatechumenal Way, colloquially known as the "Kikos." This lay movement sprang up from extremely poor neighborhoods and the work of Spaniard Francisco "Kiko" Argüello. Its forms and systems are similar to evangelical Protestantism, but its doctrinal base is clearly traditional, conservative Catholic.

The Colombian archbishop José Octavio Ruiz, closely aligned with efforts to halt the decline of Catholicism in Latin America, was named secretary of the Pontifical Council for Promoting the New Evangelization (PCPNE).

The whole idea originated with the priest Luigi Guissani, founder of the Communion and Liberation Movement. Guissani was one of the toughest fighters against Protestants in Latin America. In his famous article "Religious Awareness in Modern Man," Guissani explained what he believed the real problem for Christianity to be: "It seems to me that the Christianity of our day has been afflicted, weakened, diluted by an influence we could define as 'protestant.' "[56]

The New Evangelism has a well-defined goal: to recover social influence and halt the declining numbers of the Catholic Church. Though the PCPNE's constitution does not touch on this matter, the guidelines to the Synod of Bishops' XIII Ordinary General Assembly state:

At the same time, some regions of the world are showing signs of a promising religious reawakening. These many positive expectations, resulting from a rediscovery of God and the sacred in various religions, are, however, being overshadowed by the phenomenon of fundamentalism which oftentimes manipulates religion to justify violence and even terrorism, a serious abuse of religion. "We cannot kill in God's name!" Furthermore, the proliferation of the sects continues to be an ongoing challenge.[57]

The emphasis of the New Evangelization as a tool to curb the spread of Protestantism rings clear in Catholic Church documents within Latin America as well.

Interfaith Dialogue

Without a doubt, one of the most notable characteristics of the new pope is his great interest in interfaith dialogue. His friendship with Rabbi Skorka, an influential leader in Argentina's vast Jewish community, is renowned. He and Skorka coauthored the 2010 book *Sobre el Cielo y la Tierra,* which addresses numerous spiritual and social issues.

Rabbi Skorka and Cardinal Bergoglio used to get together twice a month. Though physical distance now makes their meetings impossible, the pope is not likely to wane in his commitment to interfaith dialogue.

The Catholic Church took a radical turn with John Paul II's arrival to the pontificate. He was also a great friend of the Jews and tried to build bridges with Islam and other religions in his famous meetings in Assisi and gatherings convened in 1986, 1993, and 1996. John Paul II's visit to the synagogue in Rome, his reception of the Muslim leader Alí Jamenei in 1998, and his retirement trip to Jerusalem confirmed this focus on interfaith dialogue. Pope Benedict XVI continued this practice, convening a meeting in 2011 with three hundred representatives of the world's different religions.

Pope Francis will follow in their footsteps.

On March 20, 2013, as he received religious leaders from other churches and religions, he said, "It is my firm intention to pursue the path of ecumenical dialogue."[58] Always in favor of dialogue, he spoke that day of the need for unity among religions in the face of all the divisions and rivalry in the world.[59]

From the very first days of his pontificate, Pope Francis has made special mention of dialogue with Jews. He sent a message to the rabbi in Rome, Riccardo Di Segni, inviting him to the papal inauguration. In this arena Pope Francis will have to revise a few changes that his predecessor made when certain pre–Second Vatican Council masses in Latin that speak against the Hebrew people were reinstituted.[60]

Muslims have also congratulated Pope Francis, despite the fact that Muslim persecution of Christians is real and on the increase over the past few decades. Practically every Muslim organization in Europe has extended congratulations to the new pope. Catholic-Muslim dialogue has been stymied for several years, especially after Benedict XVI's polemical speech in Ratisbona, in which he paraphrased a Byzantine criticizing Mohammad.

In many instances, especially regarding

celibacy, homosexual marriage, abortion, women in the priesthood, transparency in Vatican affairs, and halting the serious problem of pedophilia, Pope Francis's postures will be similar to those of his predecessors. The question remains, what is Pope Francis's agenda? How will his Jesuit background influence the way he organizes the Church? What will the Church do in the face of globalization and social networking? How will Pope Francis combine his care for the poor with an often ostentatious hierarchy?

THE FIRST POPE
FROM THE AMERICAS

We could say that the papacy has always been a very Roman, very Italian, and very European form of government. Of the 266 popes who have served in Christianity's two millennia, only forty-eight were not Italian. The reason is obvious. The pope continues to be the bishop of Rome, and, as such, it only makes sense that the people of Rome would elect an Italian, especially in the years when the Romans and later their patriciate had to ratify the appointment of the new pontiff.

In pontifical history there have been six periods when the popes were not Italian:

1. The Greek Period (97–418). In this first Greek period the influence of Greek culture and its sway over Rome were very evident. After the division of the Roman Empire, the Eastern Roman Empire, united under a sole emperor, exercised great influence over the West.

During this period, there were thirteen non-Italian popes. The majority were Greek; then there were two Africans, one Syrian, one from Dalmatia, and one Spaniard. St. Evaristus (97–105), St. Telesphorus (125–136), St. Hyginus (136–140), St. Eleuterus (175–189), St. Anterus (235), St. Sixtus II (257–258), St. Eusebius (309), and St. Zosimus (417–418) were the popes of Greek origin.

The African popes were St. Victor I (189–199) and St. Melchiades (311–314). St. Anicetus (155–166) was the Syrian pope, St. Caius (283–296) was from Dalmatia, and St. Damasus I (366–384) was the Spanish pope.

2. The Syrian Period (685–705). In this period, following a very long era without foreign popes, popes of

Greek and moreover Syrian background began to influence Rome. In this second group of non-Italians, there were five Syrian and three Greek popes. Eastern influence was very strong throughout the first eight centuries of church history.

John V (685–686), St. Sergius I (687–701), Sisinnius (708), Constantine (708–715), and St. Gregory III (731–741) were all from Syria. The Greek popes were Theodore I (642–649), Conon (686–687), and John VI (701–705).

3. The German Period (996–1075). Popes of German background dominated this period, mainly due to the power and influence of the Ottonian dynasty, a dynasty of German kings who tried to impose papal candidates favorable to their empire. During this period, there were five German popes: Gregory V (996–999), Clement II (1046–1047), Damasus II (1048), St. Leo IX (1049–1054), and Victor II (1055–1057).

4. The French Period (1057–1378). This was the longest non-Italian

period, influenced by the thriving French culture. During this time, the Pontifical See was transferred from Rome to Avignon, which partly explains the proliferation of French popes. There were a total of fourteen French popes during this period, one English pope, and one Portuguese pope.

The French popes were Stephen IX (1057–1058), Nicholas II (1059–1061), the Blessed Urban II (1088–1099), Urban IV (1261–1264), Clement IV (1265–1268), the Blessed Innocent V (1276), Martin IV (1281–1285), Clement V (1305–1314, first pope at Avignon), John XXII (1316–1334), Benedict XII (1335–1342), Clement VI (1342–1352), Innocent VI (1352–1362), the Blessed Urban V (1362–1370), and Gregory XI (1371–1378).

Adrian IV (1154–1159) has been the only English pope so far, and John XXI (1276–1277) has been the only Portuguese pope.

5. The Spanish Period (1455–1523). After the return of the Pontifical See to Rome, there was another

long period of Roman popes broken up by a few Spanish popes or popes imposed by Spain.

These popes were Callixtus III (1455–1458), Alexander VI (1492–1503), and Adrian VI (1522–1523), who was from the Netherlands.

6. The Central European Period (1455–2013). In this period all the popes were Italian until 1975, when the first Polish pope, John Paul II (1975–2005) was elected. He was followed by a German pope, Benedict XVI (2005–2013).

These six periods of non-Italian popes were characterized by influences, many times political, outside Rome. The last period has been influenced by the attempt to globalize the papacy. The Catholic Church saw the need for Catholics around the world to identify with the pope, and it recognized that a religious person from any part of the world could assume the papacy.

It might be that we are now entering the American Period. Pope Francis is the first pope from the Americas, but the trend could continue for much longer. The reasons for the shift are multiple, and some members of the Curia and high-ranking officials of the Catholic Church have already pointed to a few of the primary factors.

As already mentioned, Europe's shrinking influence in Catholicism is at play. The archbishop of Miami in the United States, Monsignor Thomas Wenski, also considers secularism as a factor behind the election of a pope from the Americas. He said, "As the focus of the population center moves away from Europe because of secularization, Latin America was a natural place for a future pope."[61]

Archbishop Wenski thinks it is a "great thing" that the new pope is Latino and believes that having an American pope will benefit the Catholic Church in both the United States and Latin America.[62] The fact that the pope is from the American continent will undoubtedly influence many Catholics currently alienated from the Church who see it as foreign and European.

Statistics explain another factor leading to the election of a Latin American pope: 40 percent of the world's Catholics, some two hundred million, live in Latin America. Of all the favored candidates at the conclave of 2013, several were from the American continent, including candidates from the United States, Brazil, Argentina, and Honduras.

Cardinal Cipriani from Lima, Peru, made it clear that within the conclave, people were asking the same question. The cardinal said, "Everyone was asking and wondering if this was the time to consider someone from Latin America."[63]

Cardinal Cipriani also pointed out that scandals within the Curia, particularly the leaking of Benedict XVI's papers, necessitated the election of a non-Italian. The cardinal went on to highlight one more reason, perhaps the most important: halting the exodus of Catholic parishioners to Protestant churches. He said,

> The sects are an answer to the vacuums and silence of the Church which at times exaggerates a series of secular discussions and forgets that it has the treasure of Christ, the treasure of faith. I think the pope is going to give us a good wake-up call regarding the treasure of the faith.[64]

An article in the *Wall Street Journal* titled "In Latin America, Catholics See a Lift" signals the geostrategic reason why a pope from the Americas might lead to the halting of the spread of Protestantism. The article discusses the hope unleashed within Latin

America at the election of an Argentine pope. It also touches on the sharp decline of Catholics in the continent, especially in Brazil, a country where now less than 50 percent of the population considers itself Catholic.[65]

Hosffman Ospino, a professor of religion at Boston College, told the *Wall Street Journal* that a Latin American pope might woo back the masses of non-practicing Catholics throughout the continent.[66]

The majority of Latin American heads of state attended Pope Francis's coronation ceremony. From the president of Argentina, who has an ambivalent relationship with the new pope, to the heads of state of Ecuador and Mexico and the president of Brazil, Latin American leaders on the whole seem very pleased with the election of a Latin American pope. In the United States, the election of a pope from the American continent might be the first bit of good news for Catholics in a very long time. The pedophile scandals have made the majority of the dioceses suspect, languishing under unprecedented media scrutiny.

What will a Latino-style Holy See look like? Will the typical Latino spontaneity and joy alter the Vatican's rigid protocol? Will Pope Francis's Latino origin draw the

Vatican closer to the people than in nearly any other period in history? Will this election change the religious map in the Americas?

Chapter 10
The First Jesuit Pope

In the end, . . . I joined the Society of Jesus, attracted by how they are a force for advancing the Church.[1]

Jorge Mario Bergoglio is the first pope from the order of the Jesuits in the entire history of the Catholic Church. It is quite rare in Catholic history for a pope to be elected from any religious order, happening only thirty-four times. Among these thirty-four popes arising from orders, the Benedictines stand out with the most popes, followed by the Augustinians, Franciscans, and Cistercians, as mentioned in the following list:

- Benedictine order: seventeen total. Gregory I, Boniface IV, Adeodatus II, Leo IV, John IX, Leo VII, Stephen IX, Gregory VII, Victor III, Urban II, Paschal II, Gelasius II, Celestine V, Clement VI, Urban V, Pius VII, and

Gregory XVI.

- Augustinian order: six total. Eugene IV; and five Canons Regular: Honorius II, Innocent II, Lucius II, Gregory VIII, and Adrian IV.
- Dominican order: four total. Innocent V, Benedict XI, Pius V, and Benedict XIII.
- Franciscan order: four total. Nicholas IV, Sixtus IV, Sixtus V, and Clement XIV.
- Cistercian order: two total. Eugene III and Benedict XII.
- Jesuit order: one total. Francis.

So why have there been so few popes from religious orders, and what makes diocesan priests more likely to reach the papacy? Religious orders have a different role than the diocesan priesthood. All orders are founded according to a particular charisma and a primary mission, whether it is care for the poor, teaching, missions, or service to some marginalized group. Religious orders have very strict rules of obedience and an internal system of hierarchy that, though unintentional, can lead to conflicts of obedience with the bishop of a particular diocese. The majority of the orders live under a strict vow of poverty, understanding the episcopacy leadership as a lifestyle far removed from their concept of poverty. Men and women in religious orders tend to avoid positions within the Catholic hierarchy, given their well-developed concept of humility.

The majority of cardinals, which are named by the pope, are from the diocesan sphere, which in turn leads them to elect people from this circle. Of all the popes with a monastic background, the majority accepted the pontificate only after much reflection since in some orders, as in the Society of Jesus, the position of cardinal or bishop is incompatible with belonging to the order.

The Jesuits are especially devoted to and only accountable to the pope, not required to obey bishops. For this task they developed a new style of compliance called anticipated obedience. Anticipated obedience means nothing more than that before a command has even been formulated, the Jesuit obeys it.

The Jesuits, despite their vow of strict obedience to the pope, were viewed with distrust by states, especially in the era of absolutism, because their independence from diocesan hierarchy made them impossible to control. The famous expulsions of

Jesuits from the majority of European states during the eighteenth century and the suppression of the order in 1773 owed largely to this mistrust of their powerful institution with significant political influence.

In 1814, after Pope Pius VII restored the Jesuit order, the Society of Jesus slowly regained part of its lost power, although suspicions of the order continued to spread. The fact that John Paul II essentially decapitated the order, placing people of his own confidence in their leadership roles as described in a previous chapter, demonstrates how hard it has always been to totally control the Jesuits.

Despite this general belief of an avoidance of positions in the hierarchy, the arrival to the pontificate of a priest with a Jesuit background has been well received by members of the Society of Jesus. Father Adolfo Nicolás, the current superior general of the Society of Jesus, elected in 2008, declared regarding Pope Francis:

"The distinguishing mark of our Society is that it is . . . a companionship . . . bound to the Roman Pontiff by a special bond of love and service." . . . Thus, we share the joy of the whole Church, and at the same time, wish to express our renewed availability to be sent into the vineyard of the Lord, according to the spirit of our special vow of obedience, that so distinctively unites us with the Holy Father.[2]

The Spanish Father Nicolás is very attentive to the poor, and in this way is in complete agreement with the new pope. Father Nicolás commented that he did not feel very close to the theological ideas of Benedict XVI,[3] a pope with an intellectual and very moderate profile.

The name of "Francis" by which we shall now know him evokes for us the Holy Father's evangelical spirit of closeness to the poor, his identification with simple people, and his commitment to the renewal of the Church. From the very first moment in which he appeared before the people of God, he gave visible witness to his simplicity, his humility, his pastoral experience and his spiritual depth.[4]

A JESUIT POPE

What does it mean for the Catholic Church to have a Jesuit pope?

The answer is up in the air. Pope Francis

could make drastic changes in the way the papacy is practiced while still maintaining the core of the Catholic Church's teaching and doctrine. His first gestures as pope reflect the Jesuit tendency of the last one hundred years: the preferential option for the poor.

In his book *El verdadero poder del servicio* (*The True Power of Service*), the pope talked about this purposeful encounter with the poor, going out to meet them where they are: "Let us search out the poorest of the poor to say with them, 'God with us.' "[5]

This focus on poverty could augment the demands the Catholic Church makes to governments and sharpen the Church's critique of the current capitalist financial structure. Pope Francis is by no means a revolutionary, but he has been very critical of the reigning system of inequality. The pope explains that this option for the poor is clearly reflected in the Second Vatican Council but has not yet been fully developed.[6] This same idea was reinforced in the 2005 CELAM conference of bishops in Aparecida, Brazil.

Despite his commitment to the poor, Pope Francis does not believe that the path of liberation theology is the one to take.[7] The fight against poverty, according to the pope, should be focused on each individual's responsibility with his or her neighbor, not on a change in the model of production.[8]

Another remarkable characteristic of Pope Francis that reflects his Jesuit training is his disregard for political power. He does not believe politics and religion should go hand in hand. Power is passing, first belonging to one group and then to another; and, the new pope believes, if the Church aligns itself with power, it will be punished.[9]

Francis claims to be as removed from communism as he is from capitalism. He sees communism as a materialist theory that holds no place for the transcendent. In capitalism he observes an extreme desire to control religion. He maintains that the Church should always have a prophetic vision that denounces injustice no matter where it originates.[10]

Upon founding the Society of Jesus, St. Ignatius of Loyola conceived the society as a militia. The resulting values of discipline and order might be the final Jesuit contribution Pope Francis brings to the Vatican. He is a man who knows how to be in charge and make sure his orders are followed. He is also not accustomed to using intermediaries; he prefers to act directly.

While archbishop of Argentina, Bergoglio

knit together a close network of assistants, people in second rank who would carry out his orders and not let things get out of control. This style will soon become more apparent, and the pope appears very willing to get the Vatican in order and choose a team aligned with his vision.

CHAPTER 11
FACING MODERNITY
AND GLOBALIZATION

> If we think of globalization as a billiard ball,
> it mows down the rich virtues of each
> culture.[1]

The new pope is unquestionably a man of the times. Unlike his predecessor, Benedict XVI, an intellectual focused on books and enamored by ancient papal ceremonies, Pope Francis is more in sync with everyday reality. In his time as archbishop of Buenos Aires, he not only traveled by public transportation but also constantly visited his many parishes, listened to people, and did not react to his position as members of the religious hierarchy typically do, only interacting with other religious leaders of the same status.

Pope Francis's down-to-earth qualities have been apparent since his election. As previously noted, by using the phrase "Bishop and People" and requesting that the people pray for him, he proved himself to be a man like any other, accessible and with his own weaknesses. This distinguishes him greatly from John Paul II who, though very close to the people, always maintained a more paternalistic attitude and upheld an image of strength and perfection that made it difficult for common people to follow his example.

This nearness to the people has solicited a wave of empathy with the pope from Argentina and throughout the Americas. On March 19, 2013, Pope Francis directly addressed the Argentine crowds gathered in the Plaza de Mayo in Buenos Aires: "Don't forget this far away bishop who loves you dearly. Pray for me."[2]

A pope this approachable will connect well with a postmodern society that is more given to feelings and emotions than ideas and thoughts. It is curious that someone with such well-defined cultural qualities can at the same time have such universal appeal. Pope Francis believes in the harmonious diversity of humanity and in a globalization that draws societies together but does not make them all uniform. He argues that imperialistic globalism ends up enslaving people groups.[3] He believes that, in globalization, a sense of identity should never be surrendered, though fusion and blending also have value. We must not forget that Pope Francis has deep European roots (his parents were Italian), but he was raised in a culturally diverse milieu.[4]

Pope Francis's ability to maneuver modern means of communication will be another key to the success or failure of his pontificate. Though Benedict XVI ended up having a Twitter account, a Facebook profile (unofficial), and a YouTube channel, he certainly never seemed very comfortable with social networking. Claudio Maria Celli, the president of the Pontifical Council for Social Communications, finally got Benedict XVI interested in social media at the beginning of 2013. The former pope reportedly preferred his Twitter account, which seemed more institutional, over a Facebook profile, which seemed too personal.[5] Despite the little activity and the institutional nature of his Twitter account, Benedict XVI had almost three million followers. In his few short weeks of having the account, he published thirty-nine tweets, very few when compared to the average tweets of a typical user.[6]

Jorge Mario Bergoglio had both a Twitter and a Facebook account, though they have since been retired, before being elected pope. On Sunday, March 17, 2013, Bergoglio wrote his first pontifical tweet, in Spanish, saying: "Dear friends, I thank you from my heart and I ask you to continue to pray for me. Pope Francis."[7] As of this writing, Pope Francis's Twitter profile has 1,258,411 followers and counting, and he has published nine tweets. The style is very realistic, making it seem that the pope himself is actually writing his tweets. Though the strict style of the Vatican will likely try to curb the pope's spontaneity, he will certainly take advantage of these means to reach out to the faithful worldwide.

CHAPTER 12
FACING THE SCANDALS
OF THE CATHOLIC CHURCH

Generally, when we talk about a double life, we mean someone who has two families. . . . But a double life is anything that makes our manner of living fraudulent, the ethical principles in our being.[1]

Religion without ethics is Pharisaism. Jesus of Nazareth constantly denounced this religious posture in his time. In that era, as today, many people hid behind religion to justify their lifestyles. Yet the Christian religion is more than rites and ceremonies. Above all it is example, ethics, and witness.

Pope Francis is very clear about the ethical dimension that must pervade the life of the church. Regardless of the social acceptability of certain behaviors, the standard is not acceptability but ethics. The financial and sexual scandals of recent years have heated up this ethical dialogue. And while the corruption is perhaps no worse now than one hundred or one thousand years ago, public opinion and mass media force leaders to take great pains in their ethical commitment. Pope Francis himself believes that concealing crimes merely prolongs the problem. Benedict XVI had declared "zero tolerance" when addressing the pedophile scandals with the bishops of the United States. The new pope seems committed to settling the problem once and for all, first by addressing the power relationships that make the victims defenseless and then through the example of holiness the Catholic Church should set.

Toward this end, the ordination of priests is very important. The decline in vocations might lead the Catholic Church to lighten their list of requirements, but that could be extremely dangerous and, in the long run, counterproductive.

As previously mentioned, Pope Francis has reportedly already expelled from the Vatican one of the men most heavily involved in concealing priest pedophiles in the United States. He seems undaunted in this regard.

Concerning the Vatileaks report that the new pope inherited, Spanish journalist and Vatican specialist Eric Frattini commented, "Pope Ratzinger knew that there were huge cases of corruption in the Vatican."[2] Frattini believes that Benedict XVI knew that he was leaving a "poisoned inheritance" for the new pope.[3]

Though no one knows what internal changes the Vatican may undergo, it is certain that Pope Francis will be decisive with his actions. The first notable signs will be changes within the secretaries of the Vatican. Pope Francis will surround himself with people he trusts. He will not want, as has happened to other popes, his instructions to go ignored. His simplicity, which makes him seem more like a parish priest than a pope, should fool no one. He is a very intelligent man who knows how to pull strings when necessary.

One step the new pope is very likely to take in this regard is to make the secret reports available to the cardinals, as cardinals from the United States had previously requested of Benedict XVI.

In many ways Pope Francis is similar to the late John Paul I — an honest, direct, congenial man who was very willing to change things. Will Pope Francis be able to institute lasting change within the core of the very obscure Vatican administration? Will he manage to depose Vatican officials who stand in the way of reform? In this regard many hope that Francis's pontificate lasts much longer than that of the late John Paul I.

CHAPTER 13
THE HUMBLE POPE,
FRIEND OF THE POOR

An encounter with God has to come from within. I must put myself in God's presence and, aided by his Word, keep going wherever he wants.[1]

In Christianity prayer is indispensable for the development and growth of the believer. Intercession and prayer are part of the dynamic of the church as a whole but also of the devotional life of each individual. Pope Francis's disposition toward prayer has been made clear: in one of his first public prayers as pope, in his first tweet, and in his address to the faithful gathered in Buenos, he has asked his listeners to pray for him.

The new pontiff appears to understand the importance of constant prayer and meditation, not as an artificial psychological aid but as a tool for day-to-day reality. That is why he believes prayer is one of the pillars of the priesthood.[2] Perhaps his most beautiful comment regarding prayer is in his definition of it as an act of liberty.[3] Pope Francis does not believe in a human attempt to control prayer. It must always be a voluntary act, not regulated by anyone or anything. Neither is prayer a way to control God or God's will, because God is fundamentally a free being with his own will. Then what does prayer do?

For the pope, prayer is essentially an act of communication, simply speaking and listening.[4] He sees in prayer a mixture of reverent silence, while waiting for God to speak, and the kind of bargaining Abraham attempted in effort to convince God. Moses also bargained with God, asking for things and imposing conditions. Prayer never ends with a person's will nor with God's will; instead, both wills seem to find each other at a certain place and walk together. Prayer is, for Francis, a mixture of courage, humility, and worship.[5] When prayer becomes a mere liturgical act or social event, we run the risk of losing the strength and hope that it brings. The pope believes, therefore, that prayer should be the center of all things.

Interestingly, Pope Francis asserts that the pull of wealth disappears with prayer because the most important thing is to give of oneself, like the widow who gave from what she did not have in her offering for the temple.[6]

The pope has written about the first time Protestants invited him to one of their massive gatherings. After a while they asked if he wanted them to pray for him. Some did not understand why he would allow people from another church to pray for him:

The first time the evangelists invited me to one of their meetings in Luna Park, the stadium was full. That day a Catholic priest and a Protestant pastor spoke. . . . At one point, the Protestant pastor asked everyone to pray for me and my ministry. . . . When they were all praying, the first thing that occurred to me was to kneel on my knees, a very Catholic gesture, to receive the prayer and blessing of the seven million people there. The next week, a magazine ran a story titled, "Buenos Aires, *sede vacante*. Archbishop Commits Apostasy." For them, praying together with others was apostasy. Even with an agnostic, from his or her place of doubt, we can look upward together and seek transcendence. Each one prays according to his or her tradition. What's wrong with that?[7]

Pope Francis believes that prayer is what unites, not separates, people. The new pope wants to receive the blessing of all people, whether they belong to the Catholic Church or not.

Prayer, as an act of humility, is what Pope Francis believes is the only defense against hypocrisy because before God, no one can lie or pretend. What was done in public is rewarded in private.[8] Humility is the only way never to lose oneself or grow apart from God. In the Bible, people were certainly imperfect, yet when they humbled themselves before God, God received them back. The pope's thoughts on hypocrisy are the culmination of his thoughts on prayer:

Spiritual hypocrisy is very common among people who take shelter in the Church but do not live out the justice proclaimed by God. Nor do they demonstrate repentance. These are the ones who, colloquially speaking, lead a double life.[9]

CONCLUSION

Jorge Mario Bergoglio is a pope for a new century. In many ways Benedict XVI was a roadblock for the Catholic Church trying to find its way toward modernity.

The papacy currently faces many complex challenges. To quote the man Catholics consider to be their first pope, St. Peter, "For the time has come for judgment to begin at the house of God; and if it begins with us first, what will be the end of those who do not obey the gospel of God?" (1 Peter 4:17). The Catholic Church needs ethical renewal to bring into the light everything that is hinted at through Vatileaks and the child abuse scandals. Yet it also needs spiritual renewal to focus its message on twenty-first-century men and women.

Jorge Mario Bergoglio faces challenges of titanic proportions: 1.2 billion faithful, thousands of priests, members of religious orders, education centers, service centers, residencies, and church buildings — they all make up the material and human legacy of the Church, but as Pope Francis has said, "if we do not profess Jesus Christ, things go wrong. We may become a charitable NGO [nongovernmental organization], but not the Church, the Bride of the Lord."[1] Putting Christ back at the center of the Catholic Church seems to be the new pope's main objective. In one sense the church is Christ and Christ is the church. The followers of Christ are to change the world with Christ's message, rather than the world changing the church.

Prayer might be the key for this seventy-six-year-old bishop of Rome with a Buenos Aires accent, a love of soccer, and a tendency to call things as he sees them. Let no one be deceived: Pope Francis is truly the first pope of the twenty-first century. As the pope himself wrote in one of his tweets: "True power is service. The Pope must serve all people, especially the poor, the weak, the vulnerable."[2]

TEN QUOTES THAT REVEAL WHAT POPE FRANCIS BELIEVES

1. The Christian people must be at the center of the Church.

"And now, we take up this journey: Bishop and People. This journey of the Church of Rome which presides in charity over all the Churches. A journey of fraternity, of love, of trust among us. Let us always pray for one another. Let us pray for the whole world, that there may be a great spirit of fraternity."[1]

2. Prayer is an instrument of service.

Prayer is a mixture of "courage, humility, and worship."[2]

3. Jesus Christ is the center of the Christian message.

"If we do not profess Jesus Christ,

things go wrong. We may become a charitable NGO, but not the Church, the Bride of the Lord."[3]

4. His style should continue to be simple and approachable.

"Don't forget this far away bishop who loves you dearly. Pray for me."[4]

5. Protecting creation is our responsibility.

"Please, I would like to ask all those who have positions of responsibility in economic, political and social life, and all men and women of goodwill: let us be 'protectors' of creation, protectors of God's plan inscribed in nature, protectors of one another and of the environment."[5]

6. Social media can be used to engage the faithful.

From Pope Francis's first tweet: "Dear friends, I thank you from my heart and I ask you to continue to pray for me. Pope Francis."[6]

7. The pope is servant to the people.

"True power is service."[7]

8. The New Evangelization can increase church growth and effectiveness.

"The Church must go out in search of the people."[8]

9. Overcoming the vocational crisis is possible.

"The so-called crisis of identity for priests threatens us all and is part of a larger crisis of civilization. But if we know how to curb its progress, we will head for deep waters in the name of the Lord and cast our nets."[9]

10. We must be wary of our emotions.

"Let us not forget that hatred, envy and pride defile our lives!"[10]

CHRONOLOGY

1936 Born December 17 in the Flores neighborhood of Greater Buenos Aires, Argentina, to a family of moderate means. His father, Mario José Bergoglio, accountant and railway worker, was from Piedmont, Italy; his mother was Regina Sivori, a homemaker. Bergoglio is the oldest of five children.

1948 Young Bergoglio has his first girlfriend, to whom he confesses that if she will not marry him, he will become a priest.

1953 At age seventeen Bergoglio stops for confession with his parish priest while on his way to a traditional celebration for the *Dia de la primavera* and receives a calling to become a priest himself.

1954 Begins studies as a chemical technician.

1957 Suffers a serious respiratory illness that permanently incapacitates one of his lungs.

1958 On March 11, Bergoglio enters the novitiate of the Society of Jesus. In this period he completes his humanities studies in Chile.

1963 Back in Buenos Aires, he obtains his advanced *licenciatura* degree in theology and philosophy at the school of philosophy of the *Colegio San José* in San Miguel.

1964–1965 Professor of literature and psychology at the *Colegio de la Inmaculada de Santa Fe.*

1966 Professor of literature at the *Colegio del Salvador de Buenos Aires.*

1970–1971 Studies at the University of Alcalá de Henares, Spain.

1973–1979 Is placed in positions of authority with the Jesuits in Argentina.

1973 Administrator of the *Universidad El Salvador.*

1980–1986 Professor at the *Facultad de Teología de San Miguel* and president of the *Colegio Máximo* of the *Facultad de Filosofía y Teología.*

1986 Finishes his doctoral thesis in Germany and returns to Argentina. Moves to Córdoba, Argentina, to serve as a spiritual director and confessor for the Society of Jesus.

1992 Is ordained auxiliary bishop of Buenos

Aires and aide to Archbishop Antonio Quarracino.

1997 Is named bishop coadjutor of Buenos Aires.

1998 On February 28, after the death of Antonio Quarracino, Bergoglio becomes the archbishop of Buenos Aires and primate of Argentina.

2001 On February 21, John Paul II names him cardinal, the titular Protector of the Church of St. Roberto Belarmino.

2001 In September, Bergoglio presides over the Synod of Bishops at the Vatican and is applauded for his work in the meeting.

2005–2011 President of the Argentine Episcopal Conference.

2005 To everyone's surprise, Bergoglio is the runner-up in the conclave that elects Benedict XVI as pope.

2013 On March 13, Bergoglio is elected to succeed Benedict XVI, becoming Pope Francis.

2013 On March 19, Francis's inaugural papal mass is held.

ECCLESIAL POSITIONS BEFORE BEING NAMED POPE

- Ordinary bishop for the Ordinariate for the Faithful of Eastern Rite in Argentina, responsible for those believ-

ers of Eastern Catholicism who have no ordinary in their region
- Grand Chancellor of the *Universidad Católica Argentina*
- Adjunct General Relator of the Synod of Bishops' Tenth Ordinary General Assembly in October 2001
- President of the Argentine Episcopal Conference from November 2005 to November 2011
- In the consistory of February 21, 2001, named by John Paul II the Cardinal Protector of the Church of St. Roberto Belarmino
- Member of the following congregations of the Curia: Congregation for Divine Worship and the Discipline of the Sacraments, Congregation for the Clergy, and Congregation for the Institutes of Consecrated Life and Societies of Apostolic Life
- Member of the Pontifical Council for the Family
- Member of the Pontifical Commission for Latin America

BIBLIOGRAPHY

Blanco Sato, Pablo. *Benedicto XVI. El papa alemán*. Barcelona: Planeta, 2011.

Bonaventure, St. *Life of Saint Francis*. London: J. M. Dent, 1904.

Cornwell, John. *Hitler's Pope: The Secret History of Pius XII*. New York: Viking, 1999.

Difonzo, Luigi. *St. Peter's Banker*. New York: Watts, 1983.

Frattini, Eric. *La santa alianza*. Madrid: Espasa, 2006 [*The Entity: Five Centuries of Secret Vatican Espionage*. New York: St. Martin's Press, 2008].

——. *Los cuervos del Vaticano*. Madrid: Espasa, 2012.

Fülöp-Miller, René. *Power and Secret of the Jesuits*. N.P.: 1930; repr. Kessinger: 1997.

García-Villoslada, Ricardo. *Historia de la Iglesia en España, III-1*. Madrid: Biblioteca de Autores Cristianos, 1979.

——. *Historia de la Iglesia en España, III-2*.

Madrid: Biblioteca de Autores Cristianos, 1979.

Guissani, Luigi. "Religious Awareness in Modern Man." *Communio* 25, no. 1 (1998): 104–40. http://communio-icr.com/articles/PDF/giussani25-1.pdf.

Hebblethwaite, Peter. *Paul VI: The First Modern Pope.* New York: Paulist Press, 1993.

Ignatius of Loyola. *Autobiography of St. Ignatius.* Edited by J. F. X. O'Conor, S.J. New York: Benziger Brothers, 1900.

Lugones, Leopoldo. *El imperio jesuítico.* Barcelona: Orbis, 1987.

Paris, Edmond. *The Secret History of the Jesuits.* Chino, CA: Chick, 1975–1982.

Rouquette, Robert. *Saint Ignace de Loyola et les origines des Jésuites.* Paris: Albin Michel, 1944.

Rubin, Sergio, and Francesca Ambrogetti. *El jesuita.* Buenos Aires: Vergara, 2010.

Walter, Wellington. *Historia de la iglesia cristiana.* Buenos Aires: La Aurora, n.d.

Ynfante, Jesús. *Opus Deí. Así en la tierra como en el cielo.* Barcelona: Grijalbo, 1996.

Published Works by Jorge Mario Bergoglio, Pope Francis

Books

Meditaciones para religiosos. Buenos Aires: Diego de Torres, 1982.

Reflexiones en esperanza. Buenos Aires: Universidad del Salvador, 1992.

Diálogos entre Juan Pablo II y Fidel Castro. Buenos Aires: Ed. Ciudad Argentina, 1998.

Hambre y sed de justicia. Buenos Aires: Claretiana, 2001.

Educar: exigencia y pasión: desafíos para educadores cristianos. Buenos Aires: Claretiana, 2003.

Ponerse la patria al hombro: memoria y camino de esperanza. Buenos Aires: Claretiana, 2004.

Educar, elegir la vida. Buenos Aires: Claretiana, 2004.

La nación por construir: utopía, pensamiento y compromiso: VIII Jornada de Pastoral Social. Buenos Aires: Claretiana, 2005.

Corrupción y pecado: algunas reflexiones en torno al tema de la corrupción. Buenos Aires: Claretiana, 2005.

Seminario: las deudas sociales de nuestro tiempo: la deuda social según la doctrina de la iglesia. Buenos Aires: EPOCA-USAL, 2009.

Bergoglio, Jorge Mario, and Abraham Skorka. *Sobre el cielo y la tierra.* Buenos Aires: Sudamericana, 2010.

Nosotros como ciudadanos, nosotros como pueblo: hacia un bicentenario en justicia y solidaridad 2010–2016. Buenos Aires: Claretiana, 2011.

Articles

"20 años después. Una memoriosa relectura del Documento 'Historia y Cambio.'" *Signos Universitarios: Revista de la Universidad del Salvador* 26 (1994): 9–20. Buenos Aires: USAL.

"La vida sagrada y su misión en la Iglesia y en el mundo." *Teología: revista de la Facultad de Teología de la Pontificia Universidad Católica Argentina* 66 (1995): 203–12.

"El camino hacia el futuro. Llevando consigo la memoria de las raíces." *Humanitas* 47 (2007): 468–83. Santiago de Chile: PUC de Chile.

Prologues

Castiñeira de Dios, José María. *El santito Ceferino Namuncurá: relato en verso.* Buenos Aires: Lumen, 2007.

Carriquiry Lecour, Guzmán. *El bicentenario de la independencia de los países latinoamericanos: ayer y hoy.* Madrid: Encuentro, 2012.

Collaborations

Ecclesia Catholica, Edward Michael Egan, and Jorge Mario Bergoglio. *Episcopus minister Evangelii Iesu Christi propter spem mundi: relatio post disceptationem.* E Civitate Vaticana: [s. n.], 2001.

Rosario: Preghiera prediletta. Rome: Nova Itinera, 2003.

NOTES

Book Opening Epigraphs

1. Sandro Magister, quoted in Sergio Rubin and Francesca Ambrogetti, *El jesuita: conversaciones con el cardenal Jorge Bergoglio, sj.* (Buenos Aires: Vergara, 2010), digital version, 9.
2. Actualidad Evangélica, "Luis Palau: 'El Papa Francisco es un hombre centrado en Jesucristo, que lee la Biblia todos los días,' " March 14, 2013, http://www .actualidadevangelica.es/index.php ?option=com_content&view=article&id =5241:luis-palau-qel-papa-francisco-es -un-hombre-centrado-en-jesucristo-que -lee-la-biblia-todos-los-diasq&catid=8 :norteamerica.
3. Barack Obama, quoted in David Jackson, "Obama sends best wishes to Pope Francis," *USA Today,* March 14, 2013, http:// www.usatoday.com/story/theoval/2013/03/ 13/obama-michelle-pope-francis/1985687.

4. Fox Deportes, "De Messi al Papa Francisco: 'Mucha luz,' " EFE News Agency, March 16, 2013, http://www.foxdeportes.com/laliga/story/messi-y-sus-deseos-al-papa-francisco.

5. Pope Francis on YouTube.com, "CARITAS Bergoglio 03/06," Asamblea Nacional Caritas 2009, Charla de Bergoglio a miembros de Cáritas Charla No. 3 de 6 partes (Bergoglio's speech to members of Cáritas, part 3 of 6, at the 2009 Cáritas National Assembly), uploaded May 25, 2009, http://www.youtube.com/watch?v=Zey5vu-UCeA.

6. Jorge Mario Bergoglio, "Desgrabación de la homilía del cardenal Jorge Mario Bergoglio SJ, arzobispo de Buenos Aires en la misa de clausura del Encuentro de Pastoral Urbana Región Buenos Aires," September 2, 2012, http://www.pastoralurbana.com.ar/archivos/bergoglio.pdf.

7. AICA On Line, "Entrevista al Card. Jorge M. Bergoglio," November 9, 2011, http://www.aicaold.com.ar/index.php?module=displaystory&story_id=29236&format=html&fech=2011-11-09.

Introduction

1. Pope Francis, "Apostolic Blessing 'Urbi et Orbi,' " March 13, 2013, http://

www.vatican.va/holy_father/francesco/
elezione/index_en.htm.

2. Pope Francis, "Audience to Representatives of the Communications Media: Address of the Holy Father Pope Francis," March 16, 2013, http://www.vatican.va/holy_father/francesco/speeches/2013/march/documents/papa-francesco_2013 0316_rappresentanti-media_en.html.

Chapter 1: The Language of His Memories

1. Pope Francis, quoted in Sergio Rubin and Francesca Ambrogetti, *El jesuita: conversaciones con el cardenal Jorge Bergoglio, sj.* (Buenos Aires: Vergara, 2010), digital edition, 19.

2. Ibid., 23.

3. Ibid.

4. Ibid.

5. Alida Juliani Sánchez, "Vecinos de la infancia del Papa recuerdan su vida . . . y su novia," *El Nuevo Herald,* EFE News Agency, Thursday, March 14, 2013, http://www.elnuevoherald.com/2013/03/14/1431312/vecinos-de-la-infancia-del-papa.html.

6. Ibid.

Chapter 2: That Spring Day

1. Pope Francis, quoted in Sergio Rubin and Francesca Ambrogetti, *El jesuita: conversaciones con el cardenal Jorge Bergoglio, sj.* (Buenos Aires: Vergara, 2010), digital edition, 33.

2. Ibid.

3. Jorge Bergoglio and Abraham Skorka, *Sobre el Cielo y la Tierra* (Buenos Aires: Sudamericana, 2011), digital edition, pos 497.

4. Rubin and Ambrogetti, *El jesuita,* 34.

5. Ibid., 33.

6. Ibid., 35.

7. Ibid., 36. Pope Francis is referring to 1 John 4:10: "In this is love, not that we loved God, but that He loved us and sent His Son to be the propitiation for our sins."

8. Rubin and Ambrogetti, *El jesuita,* 28.

9. Ibid.

10. Ibid.

11. Ibid., 40.

12. Ibid., 38.

13. Bergoglio and Skorka, *Sobre el Cielo y la Tierra,* pos 497.

14. Ibid.

Chapter 3: Difficult Days of Dictatorship

1. Jorge Bergoglio and Abraham Skorka, *Sobre el Cielo y la Tierra* (Buenos Aires: Sud-

americana, 2011), digital edition, pos 1402.

2. *Humani generis* was an encyclical written by Pius XII on August 12, 1950, against the theology of supporting the working class.

3. Pope Francis, quoted in Sergio Rubin and Francesca Ambrogetti, *El jesuita: conversaciones con el cardenal Jorge Bergoglio, sj.* (Buenos Aires: Vergara, 2010), digital edition, 106.

4. Rubin and Ambrogetti, *El jesuita,* 107.

5. Ibid.

6. Ibid.

7. Ibid., 108.

8. Ibid.

9. Ibid.

10. Elmundo.com, "El papa Francisco será ¿peronista?" Diario El Mundo, March 14, 2013, http://elmundo.com.sv/el-papa -francisco-sera-peronista.

11. William Neuman, " 'Dirty War' Victim Rejects Pope's Connection to Kidnapping," *New York Times,* March 21, 2013, http://www.nytimes.com/2013/03/22/ world/americas/jesuit-priest-rejects-popes -connection-to-kidnapping.html?_r=0.

12. Jorge Bergoglio and Abraham Skorka, *Sobre el Cielo y la Tierra* (Buenos Aires:

Sudamericana, 2011), digital edition, pos 275.

Chapter 4: The Ascent of a Humble Man

1. Noticias de Cuyo blog, " 'El best seller de mi vida lo escribe Dios' dijo el Nuevo papa," March 13, 2013, http://noticiasdecuyo.wordpress.com/2013/03/13/el-best-seller-de-mi-vida-lo-escribe-dios-dijo-el-nuevo-papa.
2. Sergio Rubin and Francesca Ambrogetti, *El jesuita: conversaciones con el cardenal Jorge Bergoglio, sj.* (Buenos Aires: Vergara, 2010), digital edition, 12.
3. Yamid Amat, "Bergoglio es un cardenal que puso la Iglesia en la calle," interview with Monsignor Enrique Eguía Seguí, auxiliary bishop of Buenos Aires, *El Tiempo,* March 16, 2013, http://www.eltiempo.com/vida-de-hoy/religion/entrevista-a-monsenor-enrique-eguia_12695313-4.
4. Rubin and Ambrogetti, *El jesuita,* 13.
5. "Pliego de preguntas a tenor del cual deberá responder el testigo Jorge Mario Bergoglio," ("Questions awaiting response from the witness Jorge Mario Bergoglio"), September 23, 2010, http://www.abuelas.org.ar/material/documentos/BERGOGLIO.pdf.

Chapter 5: The Jesuits

1. Ignatius of Loyola, *Autobiography of St. Ignatius,* ed. J. F. X. O'Conor, SJ (New York: Benziger Brothers, 1900), 27–28.

2. Jesuitas.es, "Biografía de San Ignacio," http://www.jesuitas.es/index.php?option =com_content&view=article&id=168.

3. Robert Rouquette, *Saint Ignace de Loyola et les origines des Jésuites* (Paris: Albin Michel, 1944), 6.

4. René Fülöp-Miller, *Power and Secret of the Jesuits* (1930; repr. Kessinger, 1997), 318.

5. John Adams to Thomas Jefferson, May 5, 1816; quoted in Fülöp-Miller, *Power and Secret of the Jesuits,* 390.

6. Charles Paschal Telesphore Chiniquy, *Fifty Years in the Church of Rome* (New York: Fleming H. Revell, 1886), 699.

7. Quoted in Paul Hoensbroech, *Fourteen Years a Jesuit: A Record of Personal Experience and a Criticism,* vol. 2 (New York: Cassell, 1911), 87.

8. Deia.com, "Dejó de ser jesuita cuando fue obispo," March 15, 2013, http://www .deia.com/2013/03/15/mundo/dejo-de-ser -jesuita-cuando-fue-obispo.

9. James Martin, "My Take: What it means for one of my brothers to become pope,"

March 14, 2013, http://religion.blogs.cnn
.com/2013/03/14/my-take-what-it-means
-for-one-of-my-brothers-to-become-pope.
10. Ibid.

Chapter 6: Supporting John Paul II in His American Ministry

1. Homily of Pope John Paul II in his second apostolic journey to Brazil, October 12–21, 1991, translated from the Spanish as quoted in Juan C. Urrea, *Los NMR en América Latina* (Chile: Paulinas, 1992), 62; available in Italian and Portuguese at http://www.vatican.va/holy_father/john_paul_ii/homilies/1991/index.htm.

2. Synod of Bishops Special Assembly for America, "Encounter with the Living Jesus Christ: The Way to Conversion, Communion and Solidarity in America," Instrumentum Laboris, Vatican City, 1997, point 46, http://www.vatican.va/roman_curia/synod/documents/rc_synod_doc_01091997_usa-instrlabor_en.html.

3. The contributions of the Conclusions to the Fifth General Conference of the Latin American and Caribbean Episcopate focused more on the need to evangelize culture than on defense against the new Protestant churches in Latin America. The document is available in English at http://

www.celam.org/aparecida/Ingles.pdf.

Chapter 7: The Potential Pope Who Ceded to the German Candidate

1. Sergio Rubin and Francesca Ambrogetti, *El jesuita: conversaciones con el cardenal Jorge Bergoglio, sj.* (Buenos Aires: Vergara, 2010), digital edition, 92.
2. http://www.merriam-webster.com/dictionary/conclave.
3. Catholic News Agency, "Vatican reveals Pope John Paul II lasts words: 'Let me go to the house of the Father,' " September 19, 2005, http://www.catholicnewsagency.com/news/vatican_reveals_pope_john_paul_ii_lasts_words_let_me_go_to_the_house_of_the_father.
4. Rubin and Ambrogetti, *El jesuita,* ibid.
5. Benedict XVI, "Mass of Possession of the Chair of the Bishop of Rome, Homily of His Holiness Benedict XVI," Basilica of St. John Lateran, May 7, 2005, http://www.vatican.va/holy_father/benedict_xvi/homilies/2005/documents/hf_ben-xvi_hom_20050507_san-giovanni-laterano_en.html.
6. Benedict XVI, "Address of His Holiness Benedict XVI to the German Pilgrims Who Had Come to Rome for the Inauguration Ceremony of the Pontificate," April

25, 2005, http://www.vatican.va/holy
_father/benedict_xvi/speeches/2005/april/
documents/hf_ben-xvi_spe_20050425
_german-pilgrims_en.html.

7. Pablo Blanco Sato, *Benedicto XVI. El papa
alemán* (Barcelona: Planeta, 2011), digital
edition, pos 6926.

Chapter 8: The Conclave of 2013

1. Benedict XVI, "Declaratio," February 10,
2013, http://www.vatican.va/holy_father/
benedict_xvi/speeches/2013/february/
documents/hf_ben-xvi_spe_20130211
_declaratio_en.html.

2. Benedict XVI, "Missa Pro Ecclesia, First
Message of His Holiness Benedict XVI at
the End of the Eucharistic Concelebration
with the Members of the College of Cardinals in the Sistine Chapel," April 20,
2005, http://www.vatican.va/holy_father/
benedict_xvi/messages/pont-messages/
2005/documents/hf_ben-xvi_mes_2005
0420_missa-pro-ecclesia_en.html.

3. Roberto Marbán, "Eric Frattini: 'Benedicto XVI ha sido un "limpiador de ba-
sura". Pasará a la historia como un Papa
revolucionario y limpiador,' " Periodista
Digital, February 11, 2013, http://www
.periodistadigital.com/mundo/europa/
2013/02/11/eric-frattini-benedicto-vati

cano-renuncia.shtml.

4. Benedict XVI, "Declaratio."

5. Andrea Riccardi, *Juan Pablo II: la biografía* (Bogotá: San Pablo, 2011), 524–26.

6. *Civiltá Cattolica* is a magazine published by Jesuits in Rome, closely tied to the Vatican.

7. Quoted in Alfa y Omega, "Ante desafíos cruciales," February 21, 2013, http://www.alfayomega.es/Revista/2013/821/05_voc.php.

8. Cavan Sieczkowski, "Who Will Be Next Pope After Pope Benedict XVI's Resignation?" The Huffington Post, February 11, 2013, http://www.huffingtonpost.com/2013/02/11/who-will-be-next-pope-benedict-resignation_n_2661803.html.

9. Ibid.

10. Philip Pullella, "Cardinal says Latin American or African pope possible," Reuters, February 17, 2013, http://www.reuters.com/article/2013/02/17/us-pope-resignation-koch-idUSBRE91G09Z20130217.

11. *El Economista,* "Posibles candidatos para sustituir al Papa Benedicto XVI," February 11, 2013, http://eleconomista.com.mx/internacional/2013/02/11/posibles-candidatos-sustituir-papa-benedicto-xvi.

12. Julio Algañaraz, "Una avalancha de más de 90 votos convirtió en Papa a Bergoglio," March 13, 2013, http://www.clarin.com/edicion-impresa/avalancha-votos-convirtio-Papa-Bergoglio_0_883711711.html.

13. Ibid.

14. Ibid.

15. "Franciscus 13 March 2013," http://www.vatican.va/holy_father/francesco/elezione/index_en.htm.

16. Pope Francis, "Apostolic Blessing 'Urbi et Orbi,' " March 13, 2013, http://www.vatican.va/holy_father/francesco/elezione/index_en.htm.

Chapter 9: The First Pope from the Americas

1. St. Bonaventure, *The Life of Saint Francis* (London: J. M. Dent, 1904), 14–15.

2. Pope Francis, "Audience to Representatives of the Communications Media: Address of the Holy Father Pope Francis," March 16, 2013, http://www.vatican.va/holy_father/francesco/speeches/2013/march/documents/papa-francesco_20130316_rappresentanti-media_en.html.

3. St. Bonaventure, *Life of Saint Francis,* 14.

4. The papal tiara is a three-tiered crown of Byzantine-Persian origin, a representative

symbol of the papacy. It is shaped like a conical cardinal's hat ringed with three crowns from which hang two ribbons, the symbol of archbishopric. This vesture is inspired by what Jewish high priests used, as described in the Old Testament.

5. John Paul I, "Angelus," September 10, 1978, http://www.vatican.va/holy_father/ john_paul_i/angelus/documents/hf_jp-i _ang_10091978_en.html.

6. Isaiah 49:14–15: "But Zion said, 'The LORD has forsaken me, and my Lord has forgotten me.' 'Can a woman forget her nursing child, and not have compassion on the son of her womb? Surely they may forget, yet I will not forget you.' "

7. Pope Francis, "Mass, Imposition of the Pallium and Bestowal of the Fisherman's Ring for the Beginning of the Petrine Ministry of the Bishop of Rome, Homily of Pope Francis, Saint Peter's Square," March 19, 2013, http://www.vatican.va/ holy_father/francesco/homilies/2013/ documents/papa-francesco_20130319 _omelia-inizio-pontificato_en.html.

8. Ibid.

9. Ibid.

10. Ibid.

11. Sergio Rubin and Francesca Ambro-getti, *El jesuita: conversaciones con el*

cardenal Jorge Bergoglio, sj. (Buenos Aires: Vergara, 2010), digital edition, 96.

12. Ibid.

13. Terra Colombia, "Los cuatro grandes retos del papa Francisco," March 18, 2013, http://noticias.terra.com.co/internacional/renuncia-y-sucesor-de-benedicto-xvi/los-cuatro-grandes-retos-del-papa-francisco,56d60eb10fd7d310VgnVCM4000009bcceb0aRCRD.html.

14. Rachel Zoll, Associated Press, "Letters: Catholic bishops warned in '50s of abusive priests," *USA Today,* March 31, 2009, http://usatoday30.usatoday.com/news/religion/2009-03-31-catholic-abuse_N.htm.

15. Michael D. Schaffer, "Sex-abuse crisis is a watershed in the Roman Catholic Church's history in America," Philly.com, June 25, 2012, http://articles.philly.com/2012-06-25/news /32394491_1_canon-lawyer-catholic-priests-catholic-bishops.

16. "El fiscal vaticano para la pedofilia reconoce 3.000 casos en ocho años," *El País,* March 13, 2010, http://sociedad.elpais.com/sociedad/2010/03/13/actualidad/1268434809_850215.html.

17. Ibid.

18. Pope John Paul II, "Address of His Holiness John Paul II to the Cardinals of the

United States," April 23, 2002, http://www.vatican.va/resources/resources_american-cardinals-2002_en.html.

19. Ibid.

20. Nick Pisa, "Vatican investigated 4,000 cases of child sex abuse in the last 10 years, U.S. cardinal reveals," February 7, 2012, http://www.dailymail.co.uk/news/article-2097643/Vatican-investigated-4-000-cases-child-sex-abuse-10-years-U-S-cardinal-reveals.html.

21. Rubin and Ambrogetti, *El jesuita,* 72.

22. Jorge Bergoglio and Abraham Skorka, *Sobre el Cielo y la Tierra* (Buenos Aires: Sudamericana, 2011), digital edition, pos 597.

23. Jill Reilly and John Hutchinson, "Pope on a bus! Francis shows he's still a man of the people as he hops on board minibus to church on his first day on the job," March 15, 2013, http://www.dailymail.co.uk/news/article-2293785/Pope-bus-Francis-shows-hes-man-people-hops-board-minibus-church-day-job.html.

24. Fox News Latino, "Pope Francis: Controversy Arises with Disgraced US Cardinal Bernard Law," March 16, 2013, http://latino.foxnews.com/latino/news/2013/03/16/pope-francis-controversy-arises-with-disgraced-us-cardinal

-bernard-law.

25. Philip Pullella, "Pope has probably not read 'Vatileaks' report yet, Vatican says," March 18, 2013, http://www.reuters.com/article/2013/03/18/us-pope-leaks-idUS BRE92H0O320130318?feedType=RSS &feedName=worldNews&utm_source =feedburner&utm_medium=feed&utm _campaign=Feed%3A+Reuters%2F worldNews+(Reuters+World+News).

26. Ibid.

27. Eric Frattini, *Los cuervos del Vaticano* (Madrid: Espasa, 2012), digital edition, 73.

28. *El Día,* "El cardenal Cipriani admite que el Vatileaks influyó para evitar un papa italiano," March 17, 2013, http://www .eldia.es/2013-03-17/internacional/ internacional15.htm.

29. Ibid.

30. Bergoglio and Skorka, *Sobre el Cielo y la Tierra,* pos 1674.

31. Ibid.

32. Ibid.

33. Ibid., pos 1779.

34. Sacred Congregation for the Doctrine of the Faith, "Persona Humana. Declaration on Certain Questions Concerning Sexual Ethics," VIII, December 29, 1975, http://www.vatican.va/roman_curia/

congregations/cfaith/documents/rc_con
_cfaith_doc_19751229_persona-humana
_en.html.

35. Congregation for the Doctrine of the
Faith, "Some Considerations Concerning
the Response to Legislative Proposals on
the Non-Discrimination of Homosexual
Persons," points 12, 11, 10; July 23, 1992,
http://www.vatican.va/roman_curia/
congregations/cfaith/documents/rc_con
_cfaith_doc_19920724_homosexual
-persons_en.html.

36. Bergoglio and Skorka, *Sobre el Cielo y
la Tierra,* pos 1209.

37. Ibid.

38. Sacred Congregation for the Doctrine
of the Faith, "Declaration on Procured
Abortion," point 5, November 18, 1974,
http://www.vatican.va/roman_curia/
congregations/cfaith/documents/rc_con
_cfaith_doc_19741118_declaration
-abortion_en.html.

39. Ibid., point 6.

40. Bergoglio and Skorka, *Sobre el Cielo y
la Tierra,* pos 1130.

41. Benedict XVI, "Apostolic Journey of His
Holiness Benedict XVI to Valencia (Spain)
on Occasion of the Fifth World Meeting
of Families, Letter of the Holy Father to
the Spanish Bishops," July 8, 2006, http://

www.vatican.va/holy_father/benedict_xvi/letters/2006/documents/hf_ben-xvi_let_20060708_spanish-bishops_en.html.

42. Centro de Investigaciones Sociológicos, "Barómetro de octubre, avance de resultados, Estudio no. 2.960, octubre 2012," 19, http://datos.cis.es/pdf/Es2960mar_A.pdf.

43. José María Vigil, "Crisis de la Vida Religiosa en Europa," CETR, http://www.cetr.net/es/articulos/sociedad_en_cambio/crisis_de_la_vida_religiosa_en_europ.

44. Lne.es, "La esperanza de vida en España es de 81,9 años," http://www.lne.es/vida-y-estilo/salud/2012/04/04/esperanza-vida-espana-819-anos/1223893.html.

45. Vigil, "Crisis de la vida religiosa en Europa."

46. Mar Ruiz, "200 sacerdotes menos cada año por la crisis de vocaciones," Ser Radio, March 18, 2012, http://www.cadenaser.com/sociedad/articulo/200-sacerdotes-ano-crisis-vocaciones/csrcsrpor/20120318csrcsrsoc_10/Tes.

47. Obras Misionales Pontificias España, "Estadísticas: Sacerdotes," 2009, http://www.omp.es/OMP/misioneros/estadisticas/sacerdotes.htm.

48. José María Iraburu, "Causas de la escasez de vocaciones," 2nd ed. (Pamplona:

Fundación Gratis Date, 2004), 2, http://www.vocaciones.org.ar/archivos/1.pdf.

49. Hervé Legrand, "Crisis de las vocaciones sacerdotales: Ayer y hoy," 1, http://www.seleccionesdeteologia.net/selecciones/llib/vol25/100/100_legrand.pdf. Originally published in French, "Crises du clergé: hier et auiourd'hui; essai de lecture ecclésiologique," *Lumiére et vie* 33 (1984): 90–106.

50. Iraburu, "Causas de la escasez de vocaciones."

51. Bergoglio and Skorka, *Sobre el Cielo y la Tierra,* pos 574.

52. Gerardo Lissardy, "La dura competencia que enfrenta la Iglesia Católica en América Latina," BBC Mundo, March 13, 2013, http://www.bbc.co.uk/mundo/noticias/2013/03/130313_brasil_america_latina_papa_conclave_iglesia_rg.shtml.

53. Carlos G. Cano, "Lutero avanza en América Latina," July 30, 2010, http://elpais.com/diario/2010/07/30/internacional/1280440809_850215.html.

54. Rubin and Ambrogetti, *El jesuita,* 56.

55. Benedict XVI, "Apostolic Letter in the Form of *Motu Proprio Ubicumque et simper* of the Supreme Pontiff Benedict XVI Establishing the Pontifical Council for Promoting the New Evangelization,"

September 21, 2010, http://www.vatican
.va/holy_father/benedict_xvi/apost_letters/
documents/hf_ben-xvi_apl_20100921
_ubicumque-et-semper_en.html.

56. Luigi Guissani, "Religious Awareness in Modern Man," *Communio* 25, no. 1 (1998): 130, http://communio-icr.com/ articles/PDF/giussani25-1.pdf.

57. Synod of Bishops, "XIII Ordinary General Assembly, The New Evangelization for the Transmission of the Christian Faith, Lineamenta," point 6, October 2012, http://www.vatican.va/roman_curia/ synod/documents/rc_synod_doc_2011 0202_lineamenta-xiii-assembly_en.html.

58. Pope Francis, "Audience with Representatives of the Churches and Ecclesial Communities and of the Different Religions, Address of the Holy Father Pope Francis," March 20, 2013, http://www .vatican.va/holy_father/francesco/speeches/ 2013/march/documents/papa-francesco _20130320_delegati-fraterni_en.html.

59. Ibid.

60. Marcelo Raimon, "Francisco quiere diálogo con los judíos desde el primer día de su pontificado," Noticias Univisión, March 17, 2013, http://noticias.univision .com/benedicto-xvi-renuncia/conclave/ article/2013-03-17/el-primer-paso-del

-papa#axzz2OOZHew9N.

61. Phil Latzman, Christine Dimattei, and Kaylois Henry, "South Florida Reaction to America's First Pope," March 14, 2013, http://wlrn.org/post/south-florida-reaction-americas-first-pope.

62. Ibid.

63. Juan Lara, "Era el momento de un Papa latino, no de Asia o África," *El Diario Montañés,* March 17, 2013, http://www.eldiariomontanes.es/rc/20130317/mas-actualidad/sociedad/momento-papa-latinoamericano-asia-201303172014.html.

64. Ibid.

65. David Luhnow and Sara Schaefer Muñoz, "In Latin America, Catholics See a Lift," *Wall Street Journal,* March 15, 2013, http://online.wsj.com/article/SB10001424127887324392804578360931371068830.html.

66. Ibid.

Chapter 10: The First Jesuit Pope

1. Sergio Rubin and Francesca Ambrogetti, *El jesuita: conversaciones con el cardenal Jorge Bergoglio, sj.* (Buenos Aires: Vergara, 2010), digital edition, 34.

2. Adolfo Nicolás, "Statement of the Superior General of the Society of Jesus on the

Election of Pope Francis," *National Jesuit News*, March 14, 2013, http://www.jesuit .org/blog/index.php/tag/jesuit-father -general-adolfo-nicolas.

3. Redes Cristianas, "Un jesuita alejado de la tesis de Benedicto XVI al frente de la orden," January 22, 2008, http://www .redescristianas.net/2008/01/22/un-jesuita -alejado-de-la-tesis-de-benedicto-xvi-al -frente-de-la-orden.

4. Nicolás, "Statement of the Superior General."

5. Jorge Mario Bergoglio, *El verdadero poder es el servicio* (Buenos Aires: Claretiana, 2007), 96.

6. Rubin and Ambrogetti, *El jesuita,* 62.

7. Ibid.

8. Jorge Bergoglio and Abraham Skorka, *Sobre el Cielo y la Tierra* (Buenos Aires: Sudamericana, 2011), digital edition, pos 1709.

9. Ibid., 1533.

10. Ibid.

Chapter 11: Facing Modernity and Globalization

1. Jorge Bergoglio and Abraham Skorka, *Sobre el Cielo y la Tierra* (Buenos Aires: Sudamericana, 2011), digital edition, pos 1610.

2. "Papa Francisco envió mensaje a miles de argentinos en la Plaza de Mayo," March 19, 2013, *El Comercio,* http://elcomercio.pe/actualidad/1552117/noticia-papa-francisco-envio-mensaje-miles-argentinos-plaza-mayo.

3. Bergoglio and Skorka, *Sobre el Cielo y la Tierra,* pos 1627.

4. Ibid., 1628.

5. Notimex, "El papa prefiere Twitter y descarta abrir una página en Facebook: 'Es demasiado personal,' " January 24, 2013, http://www.20minutos.com.mx/noticia/1568/0/papa-benedicto/facebook-pagina/twitter.

6. Vatican News Service, "Number of Twitter followers of @Pontifex goes over the three million mark," http://www.news.va/en/news/number-of-twitter-followers-of-pontifex-goes-over.

7. Pope Francis, @Pontifex, https://twitter.com/Pontifex, March 17, 2013.

Chapter 12: Facing the Scandals of the Catholic Church

1. Sergio Rubin and Francesca Ambrogetti, *El jesuita: conversaciones con el cardenal Jorge Bergoglio, sj.* (Buenos Aires: Vergara, 2010), digital edition, 64.

2. Lasexta.com, "Eric Frattini: 'El informe

"Vatileaks" es una herencia venenosa de Ratzinger para Francisco,' " La Sexta, March 16, 2013, http://www.lasexta.com/programas/sexta-noche/eric-frattini -informe-vatileaks-herencia-venenosa -ratzinger-francisco_2013031600130 .html.

3. Ibid.

Chapter 13: The Humble Pope, Friend of the Poor

1. Sergio Rubin and Francesca Ambrogetti, *El jesuita: conversaciones con el cardenal Jorge Bergoglio, sj.* (Buenos Aires: Vergara, 2010), digital edition, 37.

2. Jorge Bergoglio and Abraham Skorka, *Sobre el Cielo y la Tierra* (Buenos Aires: Sudamericana, 2011), digital edition, pos 504.

3. Ibid., pos 624.

4. Ibid.

5. Ibid.

6. Ibid., pos 667.

7. Pope Francis, quoted in "En sus palabras: ideas que iluminan el papado de Francisco," *La Nación,* March 17, 2013, http://www.lanacion.com.ar/1564044-en -sus-palabras-ideas-que-iluminan-el -papado-de-francisco.

8. Bergoglio and Skorka, *Sobre el Cielo y la Tierra,* pos 694.

9. Ibid., pos 729.

Conclusion

1. Pope Francis, " 'Missa Pro Ecclesia' with the Cardinal Electors, Homily of the Holy Father Pope Francis," March 14, 2013, http://www.vatican.va/holy_father/francesco/homilies/2013/documents/papa-francesco_20130314_omelia-cardinali_en.html.
2. Pope Francis, @Pontifex, https://twitter.com/Pontifex, March 19, 2013.

Ten Quotes That Reveal What Pope Francis Believes

1. Pope Francis, "Apostolic Blessing 'Urbi et Orbi,' " March 13, 2013, http://www.vatican.va/holy_father/francesco/elezione/index_en.htm.
2. Phrase taken from Jorge Bergoglio and Abraham Skorka, *Sobre el Cielo y la Tierra* (Buenos Aires: Sudamericana, 2011), digital edition, pos 504.
3. Pope Francis, " 'Missa Pro Ecclesia' with the Cardinal Electors, Homily of the Holy Father Pope Francis," March 14, 2013, http://www.vatican.va/holy_father/francesco/homilies/2013/documents/papa-francesco_20130314_omelia-cardinali_en.html.

4. "Papa Francisco envió mensaje a miles de argentinos en la Plaza de Mayo," March 19, 2013, *El Comercio,* http:// elcomercio.pe/actualidad/1552117/noticia -papa-francisco-envio-mensaje-miles -argentinos-plaza-mayo.

5. Pope Francis, "Mass, Imposition of the Pallium and Bestowal of the Fisherman's Ring for the Beginning of the Petrine Ministry of the Bishop of Rome, Homily of Pope Francis, Saint Peter's Square," March 19, 2013, http://www.vatican.va/ holy_father/francesco/homilies/2013/ documents/papa-francesco_20130319 _omelia-inizio-pontificato_en.html.

6. Pope Francis, @Pontifex, https:// twitter.com/Pontifex, March 17, 2013.

7. Pope Francis, @Pontifex, https:// twitter.com/Pontifex, March 19, 2013.

8. Sergio Rubin, "Desafíos: reformar la Iglesia y sacar al Vaticano del ojo de la tormenta," El Clarín, March 20, 2013, http:// www.clarin.com/mundo/Desafios-refor mar-Iglesia-Vaticano-tormenta_0_8861 11442.html.

9. "Las cinco frases del Papa Francisco para acercar los sacerdotes a los fieles," March 28, 2013, http://www.lacapital.com.ar/ informacion-gral/Las-cinco-frases-del -Papa-Francisco-para-acercar-los-sacer

dotes-a-los-fieles-20130328-0038.html.

10. Pope Francis, "Mass, Imposition of the Pallium and Bestowal of the Fisherman's Ring for the Beginning of the Petrine Ministry of the Bishop of Rome, Homily of Pope Francis, Saint Peter's Square," March 19, 2013, http://www.vatican.va/ holy_father/francesco/homilies/2013/ documents/papa-francesco_20130319 _omelia-inizio-pontificato_en.html.

ABOUT THE AUTHOR

Mario Escobar has a master's degree in modern history and has written numerous books and articles that delve into the depths of church history, the struggle of sectarian groups, and the discovery and colonization of the Americas. Escobar is passionate about history and its mysteries, and his works cover the Inquisition and the Protestant Reformation as well as religious sects. He is also a contributing columnist in various publications. Escobar specializes in the lives of unorthodox Spaniards and Americans and resides in Madrid, Spain. For more information, visit his Spanish website at www .marioescobar.es.

The employees of Thorndike Press hope you have enjoyed this Large Print book. All our Thorndike, Wheeler, and Kennebec Large Print titles are designed for easy reading, and all our books are made to last. Other Thorndike Press Large Print books are available at your library, through selected bookstores, or directly from us.

For information about titles, please call:
(800) 223-1244

or visit our Web site at:
http://gale.cengage.com/thorndike

To share your comments, please write:
Publisher
Thorndike Press
10 Water St., Suite 310
Waterville, ME 04901